Part ▶ **3:** Working with Word Documents

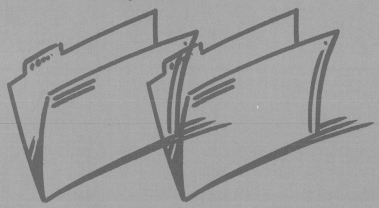

Part ▶ **4:** Word 97 Tables

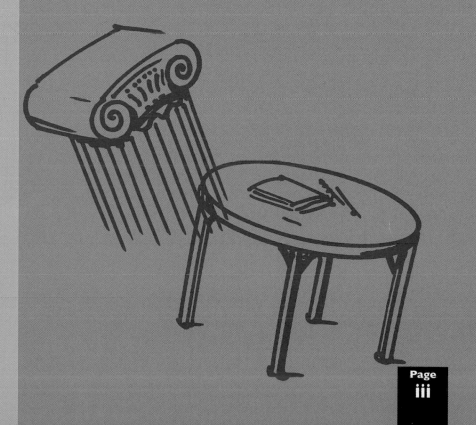

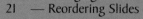

Copyright© 1998 by Que® Publishing

Library of Congress Catalog No.: 98-84854

ISBN: 0-7897-1687-9

01 00 99 98   6 5 4 3 2

Interpretation of the printing code: The rightmost double-digit number is the year of the book's printing; the rightmost single-digit number, the number of the book's printing. For example, a printing code of 98-1 shows that the first printing of the book occurred in 1998.

Trademarks

All terms mentioned in this book that are known to be trademarks or service marks have been appropriately capitalized. Que cannot attest to the accuracy of this information. Use of a term in this book should not be regarded as affecting the validity of any trademark or service mark.

Screen reproductions in this book were created using Collage Plus from Inner Media, Inc., Hollis, NH.

About the Author

Nancy Warner is a private consultant in the computer and publishing arenas currently focusing on freelance writing and development editing. She graduated from Purdue University in Computer Information Systems and has worked as an end user specialist and data access analyst. Along with the numerous computer books she has developed and edited, she has written or contributed to *Special Edition Using Office 97, Platinum Edition Using Office 97, 10 Minute Guide to Office 97, Easy Windows NT Workstation 4.0, and How to Use Access 97.*

Dedication

The dedication goes out to my husband Scott for all his love and support. Thanks again for the trip to Parker—I needed it!

Acknowledgments

I would like to express my great appreciation to Jamie Milazzo who saw me through every step of this project. Things got crazy for a while, but we made it! I would also like to thank Jim Grey for his terrific development and technical edit on this book, especially on such short notice. In addition, a huge thank you to Karen Walsh, who helped answer all my questions and put the finishing touches on this project! And last but not least, thanks to Malinda McCain. I really appreciate all your attention to detail—you caught some really good ones!

Executive Editor
Jim Minatel

Acquisitions Editor
Jamie Milazzo

Development Editor
Jim Grey

Technical Editor
Jim Grey

Managing Editor
Thomas F. Hayes

Project Editor
Karen A. Walsh

Copy Editor
Malinda McCain

Indexer
Tim Wright

Book Designer
Jean Bisesi

Cover Designer
Anne Jones

Production Designer
Lisa England

Proofreader
Betsy Deeter

How to Use This Book

It's as Easy as 1-2-3

Each part of this book is made up of a series of short, instructional lessons, designed to help you understand basic information that you need to get the most out of your computer hardware and software.

Click: Click the left mouse button once.

Double-click: Click the left mouse button twice in rapid succession.

Right-click: Click the right mouse button once.

Pointer Arrow: Highlights an item on the screen you need to point to or focus on in the step or task.

Selection: Highlights the area onscreen discussed in the step or task.

Click & Type: Click once where indicated and begin typing to enter your text or data.

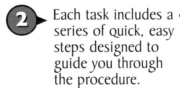

Tips and Warnings give you a heads-up for any extra information you may need while working through the task.

2 Each task includes a series of quick, easy steps designed to guide you through the procedure.

How to Drag: Point to the starting place or object. Hold down the mouse button (right or left per instructions), move the mouse to the new location, and then release the button.

Drag

Drop

1 Each step is fully illustrated to show you how it looks onscreen.

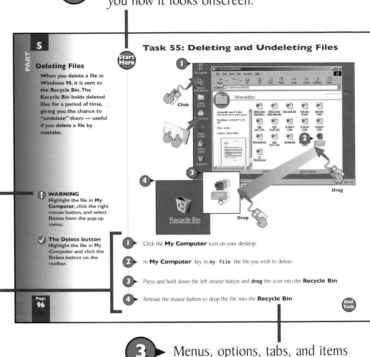

Task 55: Deleting and Undeleting Files

Deleting Files

When you delete a file in Windows 98, it is sent to the Recycle Bin. The Recycle Bin holds deleted files for a period of time, giving you the chance to "undelete" them — useful if you delete a file by mistake.

! WARNING
Highlight the file in **My Computer**, click the right mouse button, and select Delete from the pop-up menu.

✓ The Delete button
Highlight the file in My Computer and click the Delete button on the toolbar.

1 Click the **My Computer** icon on your desktop.

2 In **My Computer**, key in **my file** the file you wish to delete.

3 Press and hold down the left mouse button and **drag** the icon into the **Recycle Bin**.

4 Release the mouse button to drop the file into the **Recycle Bin**.

3 Menus, options, tabs, and items you click or press are shown in **bold**.

Next Step: If you see this symbol, it means the task you're working on continues on the next page.

End Task: Task is complete.

Introduction to Office 97

Easy Microsoft Office 97, Second Edition will help you learn the tasks to work efficiently and effectively in Microsoft Office 97 applications. More specifically, you will learn about each of the following software applications:

- *Word.* This word processing program has features that enable you to create a one-page memo, a newsletter with graphics, or a 500-page report.

- *Excel.* This powerful yet easily managed spreadsheet program can be used to generate impressive financial statements, charts, and graphs.

- *PowerPoint.* This presentation program enables you to create exciting slides and printouts that will help you give a memorable and informative presentation.

- *Outlook.* This programs provides you with an electronic mail client, daily planner, calendar, contacts list, and to-do list that helps you manage your time and projects.

Because Microsoft Office 97 is an integrated suite, you will find that many of the tasks that you learn in this book apply to other applications in the suite. For example, the formatting features in Word will apply to formatting text in Excel, PowerPoint, and in many cases even Outlook.

Tell Us What You Think!

As the reader of this book, you are our most important critic and commentator. We value your opinion and want to know what we're doing right, what we could do better, what areas you'd like to see us publish in, and any other words of wisdom you're willing to pass our way.

As the Executive Editor for the General Desktop Applications team at Macmillan Computer Publishing, I welcome your comments. You can fax, email, or write me directly to let me know what you did or didn't like about this book—as well as what we can do to make our books stronger.

Please note that I cannot help you with technical problems related to the topic of this book, and that due to the high volume of mail I receive, I might not be able to reply to every message.

When you write, please be sure to include this book's title and author as well as your name and phone or fax number. I will carefully review your comments and share them with the author and editors who worked on the book.

Fax: 317-817-7448

Email: Office@mcp.com

Mail: Executive Editor

General Desktop Applications

Macmillan Computer Publishing

201 West 103rd Street

Indianapolis, IN 46290 USA

Office 97 Basics

Part I introduces you to Microsoft Office basics. You need to know some fundamental things about Microsoft Office before you start working with its applications.

Ensure that Microsoft Office is installed on your hard disk so it appears in your Windows Programs menu. To install Microsoft Office, follow the installation instructions on disk and onscreen.

The tasks in this part are common to all Microsoft Office applications. If you learn how to perform these tasks in Word and Excel, you can perform them the same way in PowerPoint and Outlook.

Tasks

Task 1: Starting a Program

Starting an Office 97 Application

A copy of each Office program icon is placed in the Programs menu by default. From this menu, you can launch any application you installed.

✓ **The Office Assistant**
If this is the first time you have opened an Office application since you installed it, you might see the *Office Assistant* on your screen. You can leave the Office Assistant open, or close it by following the Closing the Assistant tip in Task 5.

⊘ **WARNING**
If a program doesn't show up in your Programs menu, it probably wasn't installed.

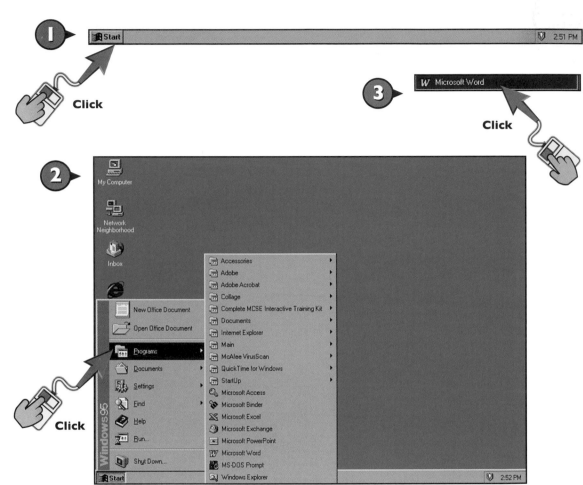

1 Click the **Start** button in the taskbar.

2 Move the mouse pointer to **Programs**.

3 Slide the mouse pointer over and click the application you want to start (for example, **Microsoft Word**).

Task 2: Selecting a Menu Command

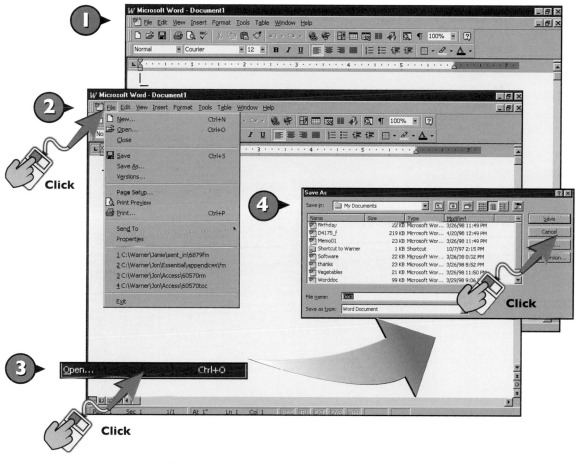

Selecting a Menu Command

The menu bar is just below the title bar. You select menu commands to perform operations such as saving a file, formatting text, or printing a document. You select a menu command the same way in all Office applications.

✓ **Menu Options**
You can access any option on a menu unless the option is grayed out, which means the option is not available for the action you want to perform.

✓ **Closing a Dialog Box**
Alternate ways to close a dialog box are to press the **Esc** key or click the **X** button in the box's upper-right corner.

1 ▸ Start Microsoft Word, using the instructions in Task 1.

2 ▸ Click **File** in the menu bar, which opens the **File** menu.

3 ▸ Click the **Open** option on the **File** menu.

4 ▸ Click **Cancel** in the Open dialog box to close the box for now.

Task 3: Using Toolbars

Using the Standard and Formatting Toolbars

To perform tasks, you can click a toolbar button with your mouse pointer, which is faster than using a menu command, especially for frequent or repetitive tasks. The Standard toolbar contains buttons for the most common commands. The Formatting toolbar contains lists and buttons for the most common formatting commands. Keep in mind that the Standard and Formatting toolbars are similar in all Office 97 applications, but not identical.

Start Here

Standard Toobar

Formatting Toolbar

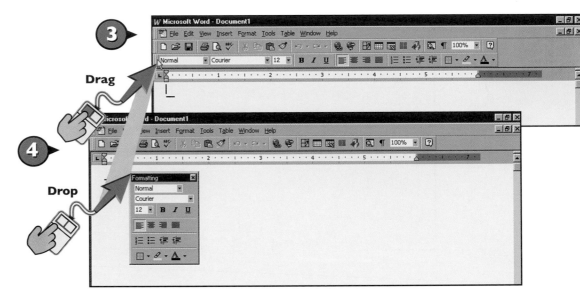

Drag

Drop

✓ **Toolbars**
You can drag any toolbar anywhere on your desktop. Notice that the toolbar's name is at the top of the toolbar after you drag it onto the desktop.

1 Move the mouse pointer over each of the buttons on the Standard toolbar. If you pause for a second, you see a descriptive ScreenTip for the nearest button.

2 Move the mouse pointer over each of the buttons on the Formatting toolbar. If you pause for a second, you see a descriptive ScreenTip for the nearest button.

3 Press and hold down the left mouse button on the two vertical bars on the leftmost side of the Formatting toolbar, and drag the toolbar somewhere on your desktop.

4 Release the mouse button to drop the toolbar in its new location.

End Task

Task 4: Using Shortcut Menus

Start Here

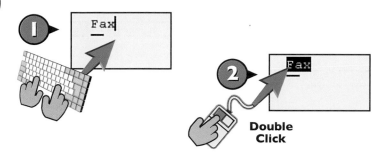

Double Click

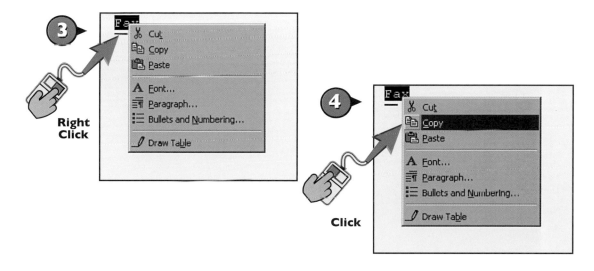

Right Click

Click

Using Shortcut Menus

Shortcut menus **include the commands you use most for whatever is currently selected—text, cells, charts, and so on. The menu's commands vary, depending on your selection. You might want to use a shortcut menu to quickly edit or format text.**

✅ **Selecting Text**
If you are having a hard time selecting text in Step 2, refer to Part 2, Task 12, for help.

✅ **Closing a Shortcut Menu**
Sometimes you display a shortcut menu that doesn't have the command you want to use. To leave a shortcut menu without making a selection, press the Esc key or click elsewhere on the desktop.

① Type some sample text (for example, **Fax**).

② Double-click the word **Fax** to select it.

③ Right-click on **Fax** to view the shortcut menu.

④ Click the **Copy** command on the shortcut menu. Word performs the action and the shortcut menu disappears.

End Task

Task 5: Getting Help

Using the Office Assistant

Office programs offer many ways to get help. The Office Assistant is a quick way to search for help on a particular topic and find shortcuts in Word, PowerPoint, Excel, and Outlook. It helps you find instructions and tips for getting your work done more easily.

Click

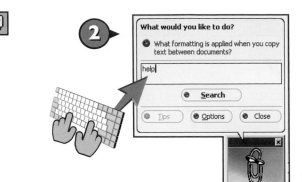

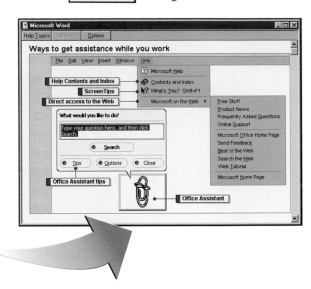

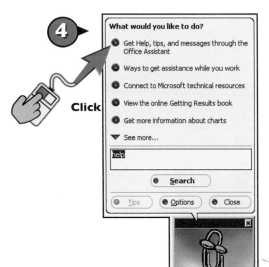

Click

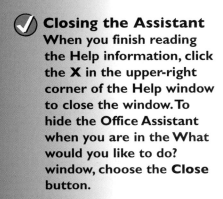

✓ **Closing the Assistant**
When you finish reading the Help information, click the **X** in the upper-right corner of the Help window to close the window. To hide the Office Assistant when you are in the **What would you like to do?** window, choose the **Close** button.

1 Click the **Office Assistant** button on the Standard toolbar.

2 Type the topic or question you want help on; for example, type **help** in the text box.

3 Click the **Search** button to view the list of Help topics.

4 Click the Help topic you want information on. The Help window appears with information about the topic you selected.

Task 6: Switching Between Open Programs

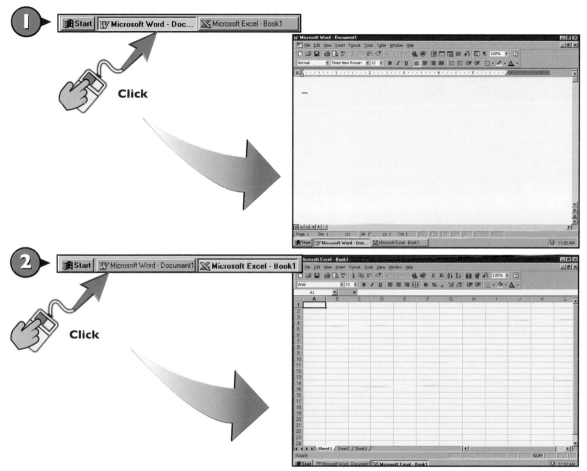

Switching Between Office 97 Applications

You can have more than one program open at a time and switch between them whenever you want. For example, you might be using data in Excel to help create a monthly report in Word, which you will immediately send to your manager by using Outlook. You can use the Windows taskbar to quickly move from one open program window to another.

✓ Resizing Application Windows
You can view multiple applications by resizing the application windows until they are each visible on the desktop. Do this by placing the mouse pointer on the window border, where the pointer turns into a double-headed arrow. Then click the left mouse button and drag the window to the desired size.

1 ▶ Click **Microsoft Word** on the taskbar. Word becomes the active program.

2 ▶ Click **Microsoft Excel** on the taskbar. Excel becomes the active program.

End Task

Task 7: Exiting a Program

Exiting an Office 97 Application

When you no longer want to work in a program, exit the application and return to the Windows desktop. The best practice is to exit all programs before you turn off your computer.

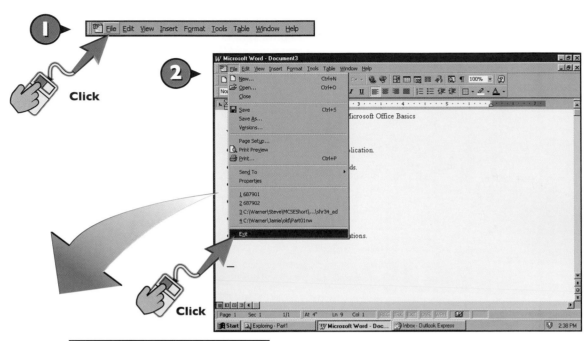

Start Here

Click

Click

Click

✓ **Taskbar**
Notice that after you close an application, the taskbar no longer has a button for that application.

✓ **Quick Close**
A quick way to close any application or window is to click the X button in the upper-right corner.

1 ▶ Click **File** on the menu bar.

2 ▶ Click **Exit** and the application closes. If you have not yet saved your work, the application asks you to save.

3 ▶ Choose the **Yes** button if you want to save your work. Choose the **No** button if you don't want to save your work. Click the **Cancel** button if you want to return to working in the document without saving.

End Task

PART 2

Word 97 Basics

Most Word documents are much larger to work with than one screen can display at a time. When you're relocating text from one area of the document to another, you must be able to move to the desired locations. To help you do this, Word provides a ruler to show your text positioning within specified margins. The ruler also shows any tabs and indents.

Word also provides information in the status bar, which tells you the exact position of your cursor within the document. For example, in a 17-page document, you might be on page 7, section 1, 3.9 inches from the top of the document, on line 14 and column 33.

The cursor shows your ***insertion point*** in a document, represented by a flashing vertical bar (I-beam) that appears in the document window. Text you type appears at the insertion point.

Any time you are working in a document, you're inserting text into that document. You use simple editing features to add text to an existing document, including Insert mode and Overtype mode (typing over text). To add text to any document, you either type new text or copy text from another document or location.

The tasks in this part teach essential skills for beginning to work with Word 97.

Tasks

Task 1: Starting Word

Getting Word Going

Word offers many features to help you create documents. Many people use Word to create letters, reports, newsletters, and faxes, but these aren't the only types of documents you can create—the best way to find out is to get started working in Word.

Start Here

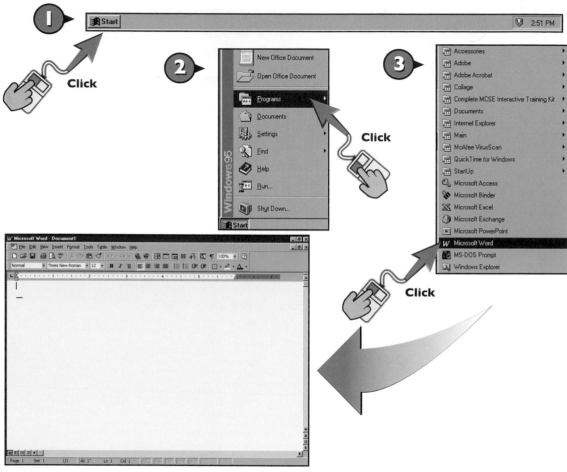

Click

Click

Click

✅ Launching Word from a File

Another way to start the Word application is to double-click a Word document file in Windows Explorer or any folder window. The application automatically launches and opens to that file.

1 ▶ Click the **Start** button on the taskbar.

2 ▶ Move the mouse pointer to **Programs**.

3 ▶ Click the **Microsoft Word** option; a new blank document opens.

End Task

Task 2: Entering Text

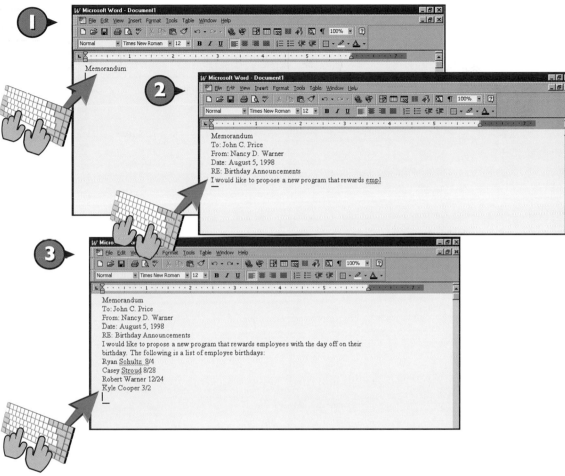

Typing Your Words

When you open Word, you can begin entering text in a document immediately. Notice that Word always begins with a default document called Document1, with the cursor at the top of the document where text you type will appear. When you have entered enough text for one line, the cursor automatically wraps (moves) to the next line. If you want to begin a new paragraph, press the **Enter** key on the keyboard.

Insert Mode and Overtype Mode
Word is in Insert mode by default—when you type, Word slides things over and inserts the text. If you press the **Insert** key on the keyboard, your typing replaces the current text (Overtype mode). The Insert key toggles Insert mode and Overtype mode on and off.

1 Type one line of text (in this case, **Memorandum**) and press the **Enter** key to begin a new paragraph.

2 Continue entering text until you are familiar with how Word displays the text onscreen.

3 Type your last line of text and press **Enter**.

Navigating Your Text

At times you want to move through your document and place the cursor in different locations to add text. You can use the mouse or the keys on the keyboard to move the cursor. This task teaches you some quick key combinations to save you time.

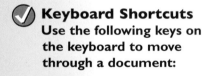 **Keyboard Shortcuts**
Use the following keys on the keyboard to move through a document:

To Move	Press
Right one character	→
Left one character	←
Up one line	↑
Down one line	↓
To the previous word	Ctrl+←
To the next word	Ctrl+→
To the beginning of a line	Home
To the end of a line	End
To the beginning of the document	Ctrl+Home
To the end of the document	Ctrl+End

Task 3: Moving Around a Document by Using the Keyboard

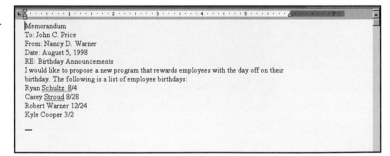

1 ▶ Press the **Ctrl+End** keys simultaneously to immediately move the cursor to the end of the document.

2 ▶ Press the up- and down-arrow keys to get the feel of how the cursor moves. Also press the **Home** and **End** keys.

3 ▶ Press **Ctrl+Home** to immediately move the cursor to the beginning of the document.

Task 4: Saving a Document

Start
Here

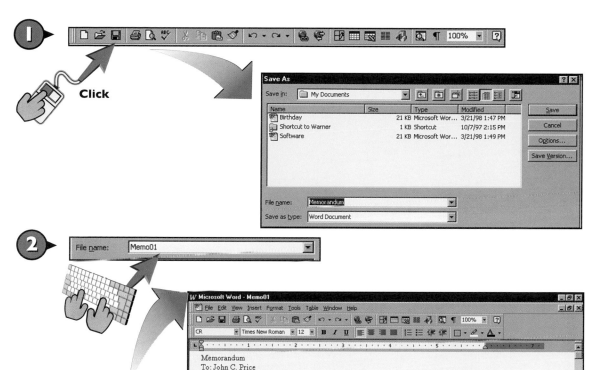

Click

2

File name: Memo01

3

Save

Click

Storing a Document on Disk

Save the document you are working in to store it on disk. A good practice is to save your documents frequently as you are working in them. After you save a document, you can retrieve it later to work on.

1 ▶ Click the **Save** button on the Standard toolbar. The Save As dialog box appears with a default filename.

2 ▶ Type a different filename if you want, for example, `Memo01`.

3 ▶ Choose **Save**. The document is saved with the filename you assigned in the title bar.

 Alternate Save-In Locations
If you don't want to save your file in the My Documents directory, you can select the Save in list box and maneuver through your directories to save your file in a different location.

Task 5: Closing a Document

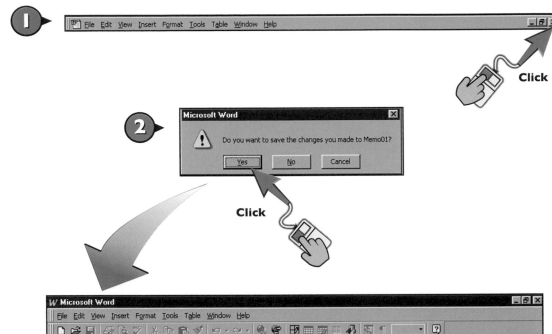

Exiting Your Work

When you finish working on a document, you can close it and continue to work on other documents. You can close a file with or without saving changes. If you have been working in a document and you try to close it, Word asks you whether you want to save the document before it closes.

✓ No Save

If you don't want to save your document when Word asks you, two options are available. If you decide you want to continue working in the document, choose **Cancel**. Or, if you want to close your document but don't want to save your changes (reverting to the previously saved document), choose **No**.

1 Click the **Close** button. If you changed the document, Word asks you whether you want to save it.

2 Click the **Yes** button if you want to save changes; Word closes the document.

Task 6: Creating a New Document

Start Here

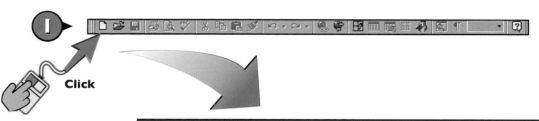

Click

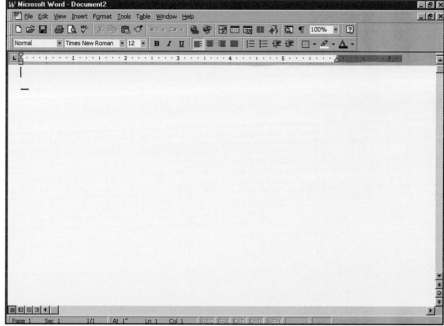

End Task

Starting with a Blank Page

Word presents a new blank document each time you start the program. You can create another new document at any time. For example, after you save and close one document, you might want to begin a new one.

Default Document Names

Depending on how many new documents you have created while you are working in Word, the default filename for each new document increases sequentially (Document1, Document2, Document3, and so on). After you exit and restart Word, the numbers begin at 1 again.

Click the **New** button on the Standard toolbar. Word opens a new document.

Task 7: Opening a Document

Returning to Saved Work

Each time you want to work with a document, you need to open its Word file by using the Open dialog box. If necessary, click the **Look in** drop-down arrow and select the folder from the list. To move up a folder level, click the **Up One Level** button on the Open toolbar. If you double-click a subfolder, its contents appear in the list of files and folders.

✅ **Alternative Open**
Another way to select a file in the Open dialog box is to double-click the filename.

✅ **Alternate Look-in Locations**
If you don't find your file in the My Documents directory, you can select the **Look in** list box and maneuver through your directories to open a file from a different location.

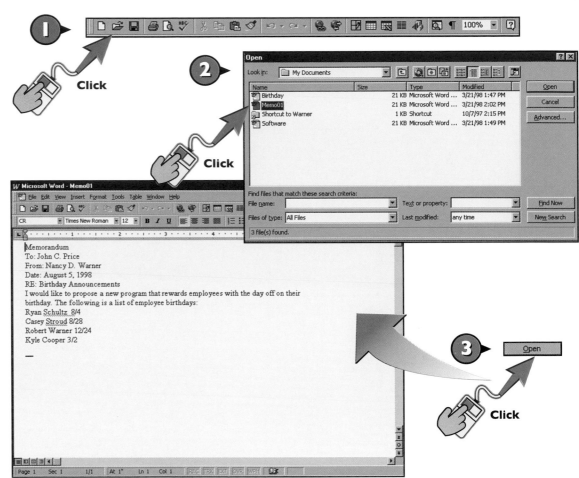

Start Here

Click the **Open** button on the Standard toolbar.

Click the file you want to open (for example, **Memo01**) in the Open dialog box.

Click the **Open** button. Word opens the document.

Task 8: Switching Between Documents

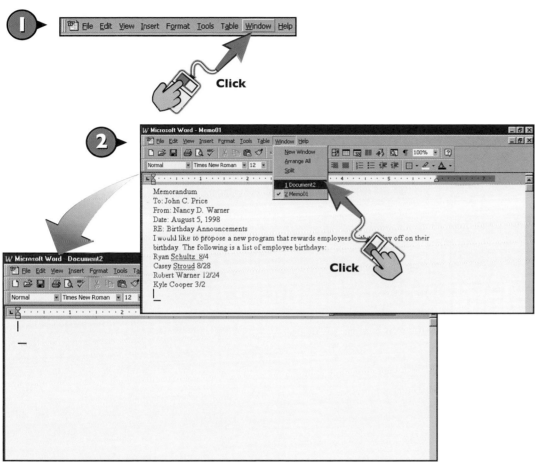

Click

Click

Keeping More Than One Document Open

When you become more familiar with working in documents, you might find it convenient to work on two or more documents at the same time. Word makes it easy to switch from one open document to another. To switch between documents, you need to have more than one document open. Task 7 tells you how to open a document.

1 Click **Window** on the menu bar.

2 Click the document you would like to switch to.

✓ More Windows
The Window menu can display only nine documents. If you have more than nine documents open, the Window menu includes a More Windows option. Choosing this option displays an **Activate** dialog box, where you can select from the list of all open documents.

Task 9: Viewing Multiple Documents

Looking at More Than One Document

If you don't want to constantly switch between documents, you can view multiple Word documents onscreen. This can be a convenient feature if you are comparing two documents or working on two documents at the same time. You can also resize each document's window. The document displaying a darker title bar is considered the *active document*; when you type, text goes there.

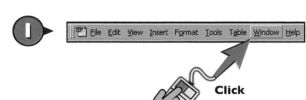

Click

Click

Click

Click the **Window** menu with the left mouse button.

Choose the **Arrange All** option.

Click on the title bar or in the body of the document you want to work in.

✓ Return to One Document

To return to viewing only one entire document, double-click the title bar of the document you want to work in.

Task 10: Changing the Document View

Start Here

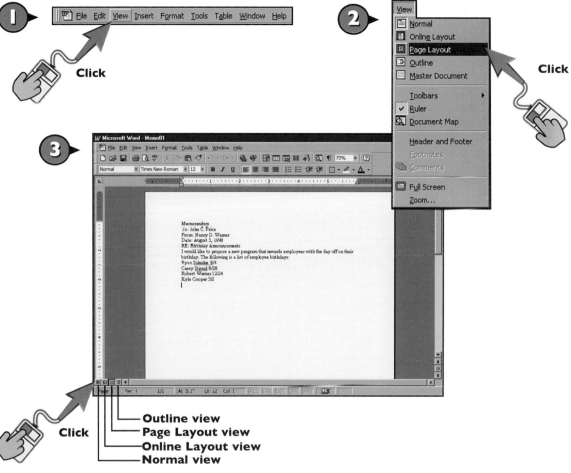

Click (1)

Click (2)

(3)

Click
- Outline view
- Page Layout view
- Online Layout view
- Normal view

Working with Views

Word provides many ways to view documents—each view has its purpose. The two most common views are **Normal** and **Page Layout**. Normal view (Word's preset view) shows text formatting in a simplified layout of the page so you can type and edit quickly. In Page Layout view, you see how objects will be positioned on a printed page.

(1) Click **View** on the menu bar.

(2) Click **Page Layout**. The document appears in Page Layout view.

(3) Click the **Normal View** button to return to the Normal view.

 Alternative Views
Other views you can select from are **Online Layout** (optimizes the layout to make online reading easier), **Outline** (shows the document's structure), and **Master Document** (organizes and maintains a long document).

End Task

Task 11: Inserting Text

Adding Words

When you insert new text into a document, Word automatically moves the existing text to the right or down a line, depending on what you type. Word also lets you insert a blank line, which moves lines down to begin another paragraph.

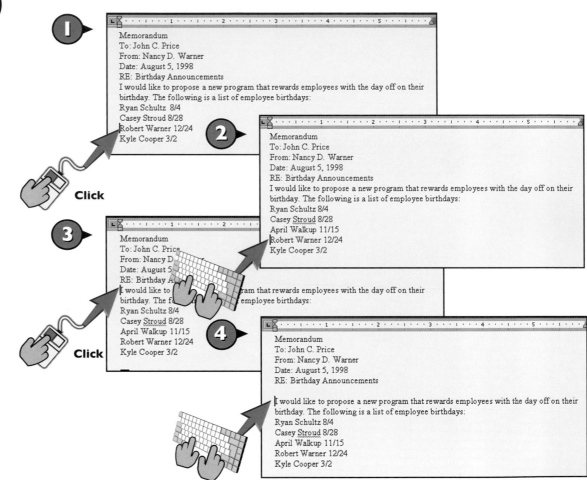

✓ Dividing Paragraphs
You can split a paragraph by moving the mouse cursor to where you want to divide the paragraph, clicking the left mouse button, and pressing Enter.

✓ Undo Changes
If you decide you don't want to insert the text you added, you can undo your insertion by clicking the Undo button on the Standard toolbar. See Task 14 for more information.

Start Here

1 Click once at the location where you want to insert new text.

2 Type the text and press **Enter**.

3 Click the cursor at the beginning of any line of text.

4 Press **Enter** to add a blank line, starting a new paragraph.

Task 12: Selecting Text

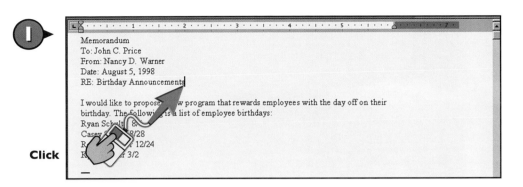

1

Click

2

Drop   **Drag**

Choosing Text to Work With

Selected text appears highlighted in the document. You select text when you want to do something to it, such as formatting, cutting and pasting, and printing.

1 Click at the end or beginning of the text you want to select.

2 While you press and hold down the left mouse button, drag the pointer over the text you want to select. Then release the mouse button.

 Select All Text
A fast way to select all the text in a document is to press **Ctrl+A**. A fast way to select an entire word is to double-click the word. A fast way to select an entire paragraph is to triple-click in the paragraph.

Task 13: Copying and Pasting Text

Using Copy and Paste

You can share information within and between documents in Word. This feature can save you time you would spend retyping or re-creating work you have already completed. For example, if you want information from the beginning of a document to appear again at the end of the document, copying and pasting the text is much more efficient than retyping it.

Start Here

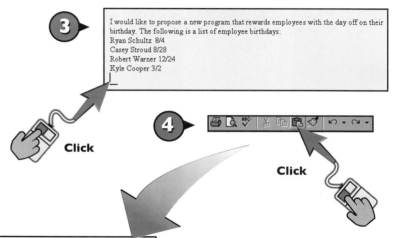

✓ **Cut Versus Copy**
When you want to move text from its current location and place it in a new location (rather than copying it), click the **Cut** button on the Standard toolbar instead of the **Copy** button. The **Cut** option actually removes the selected text from the old location.

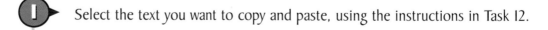

1 Select the text you want to copy and paste, using the instructions in Task 12.

2 Click the **Copy** button on the Standard toolbar.

3 Click to place the cursor in the document where you want to paste the text.

4 Click the **Paste** button on the Standard toolbar.

End Task

Task 14: Undoing and Redoing Changes

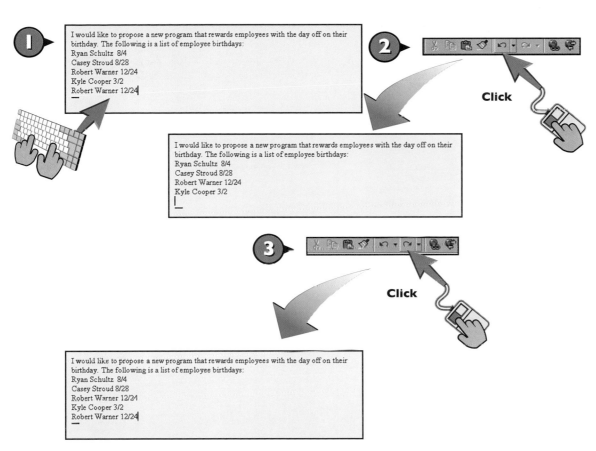

Click

Click

Fixing Mistakes

At times, you make changes to text and then decide you don't want the change after all—maybe you made a mistake, or maybe you are experimenting with your document. Whatever the reason, instead of starting over, you can undo and redo your changes. Undo and Redo are convenient when you want to see how your document looks with and without the change.

1 Type some text into a document.

2 Click the **Undo** button on the Standard toolbar; the text disappears.

3 Click the **Redo** button on the Standard toolbar; the text reappears.

✔ **Multiple Undo**
You can click the **Undo** button multiple times to undo changes as far back as when you first opened or created the document. In addition, you can click the Redo button multiple times after you have used Undo multiple times.

Task 15: Overwriting and Deleting Text

Removing Needless Text

At times, you need to alter or delete text in a document. You do this in many different ways in Word. A couple of the easiest ways are to overwrite text or to delete it with the **Delete** command. Overwriting replaces the existing text with new text as you type. Deleting completely removes the text from the document.

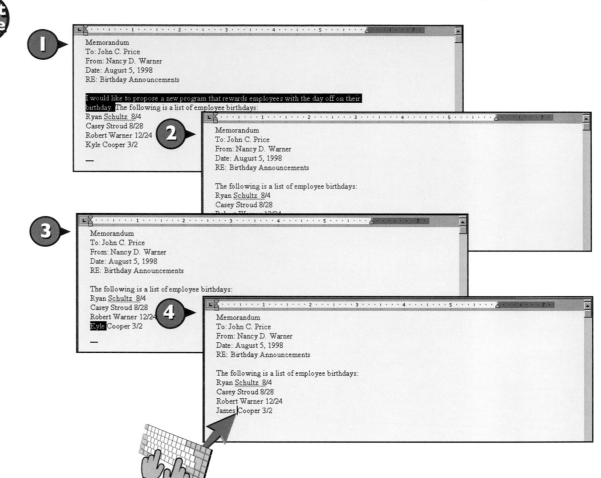

Start Here

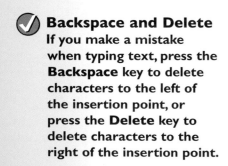

Backspace and Delete
If you make a mistake when typing text, press the **Backspace** key to delete characters to the left of the insertion point, or press the **Delete** key to delete characters to the right of the insertion point.

1 Select the text you want to copy and paste, using the instructions in Task 12.

2 Press the **Delete** key to remove the text.

3 Select the text you want to copy and paste, using the instructions in Task 12.

4 Type the text with which you want to overwrite the previous text.

End Task

Task 16: Finding Text

Start Here

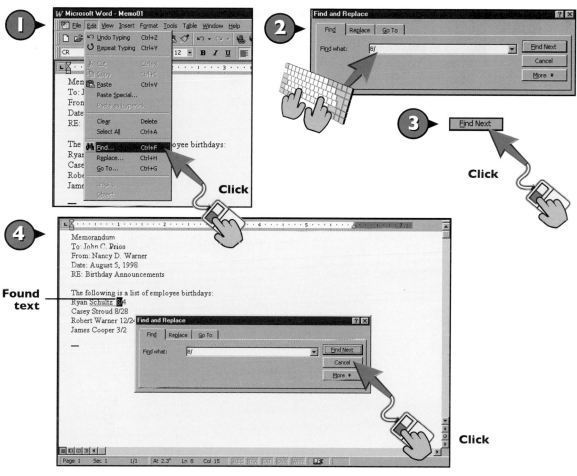

Found text

Searching for Text

You can use Word's **Find** feature to locate text, characters, paragraph formatting, or even special characters. For example, if you want to determine where your document referred to a specific name or date, you can search for that text and Word will take you to the location in the document.

Click

Click

Click

---

① Open the **Edit** menu and click the **Find** option.

② In the Find and Replace dialog box click in the **Find what** text box and type the text you want to locate.

③ Choose **Find Next** to search for the specified text. Word searches for the specified text and highlights it in the document if it is found.

④ Choose **Cancel** if you want to cancel the search.

✓ Search Item Not Found
If Word cannot find the text you are searching for, a message appears, telling you the search item was not found. Choose **OK** to resume working in the document.

End Task

Task 17: Replacing Text

Using Find and Replace

In Word, you can replace text, character and paragraph formatting, and special characters. Use the **Replace** command to have Word search for and replace all occurrences of a particular criterion. For example, if you spelled your manager's name incorrectly throughout a document, search for the misspelled name and replace it with the correct spelling.

✅ Find and Replace Dialog Box

You can search and replace through a document one occurrence at a time by clicking the **Replace** button. If you don't want to replace a specific occurrence, click the **Find** button to move to the next occurrence.

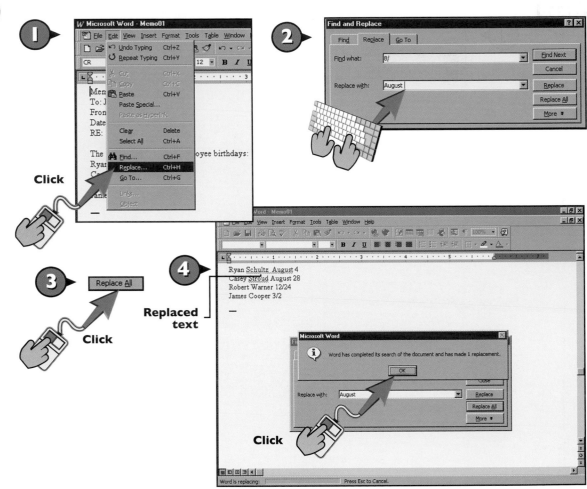

Click

Replaced text

Click

Click

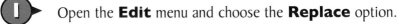

1 ▶ Open the **Edit** menu and choose the **Replace** option.

2 ▶ In the Find and Replace dialog box click in the **Find What** text box and type the text you want to locate. Then click in the Replace with text box and type the text you want to replace it with.

3 ▶ Choose **Replace All** to search and replace all the occurrences that satisfy the specified criterion.

4 ▶ Choose **OK** when Word tells you how many replacements were made. Then press **Esc** to close the Find and Replace dialog box.

Task 18: Moving Text

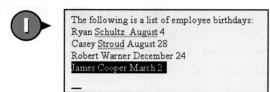

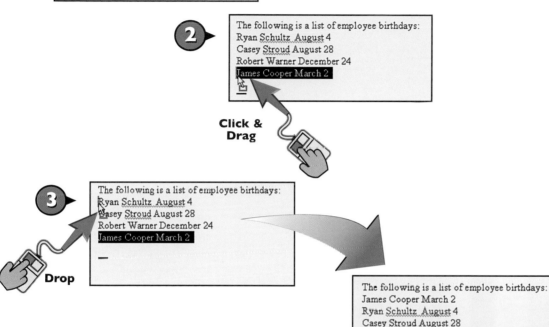

Click & Drag

Drop

Rearranging Your Words

You can reorganize text in a Word document by moving items as you work. This method is faster than cutting and pasting text. For example, if you are working on a report, you might play around with the order in which you present information. By moving instead of copying the text, you don't have to go to the new location, enter the same text, and then erase the text from the old location.

---

1 Select the text you want to move, using the instructions in Task 12.

2 Press and hold down the left mouse button over the selected text, and drag the pointer to the new location.

3 Release the mouse button to drop the text in the new location.

✓ **Undo Actions**
If you accidentally release the mouse button before you place the insertion point at your desired location, click the **Undo** button to remove the inserted text. Then try the **Move** command again.

Task 19: Checking Spelling and Grammar

Making Sure Your Text Is Well Written

Word 97 shows red wavy lines under any words it thinks are misspelled and green wavy lines under any sentences it finds grammatically problematic. This way, you immediately see if a word you typed is misspelled or a sentence is not grammatically correct.

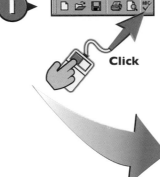

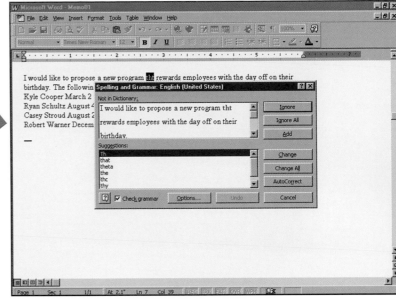

Click

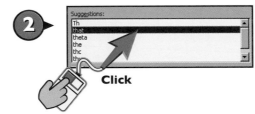

Click

✓ Not in Dictionary
If the correction for the text Word finds to be in error is not one of the options in the **Suggestions** list box, you can correct the word yourself. Click in the **Not in Dictionary** list box, type the specific correction, and choose **Change**.

1 ▶ Click the **Spelling and Grammar** button on the Standard toolbar. The Spelling and Grammar dialog box opens, displaying the first spelling or grammar error it finds.

2 ▶ Click the appropriate option in the **Suggestions** list box.

3 ▶ Choose **Change**. Word makes the change in the document and moves to the next error it finds.

Next Step

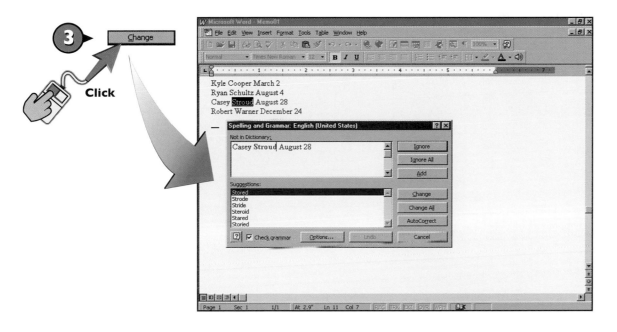

Check from the Beginning

You don't have to be at the beginning of a document when you check for spelling and grammar errors. If you start in the middle of a document, Word checks until it reaches the end and then automatically asks you whether you want to continue checking at the beginning of your document.

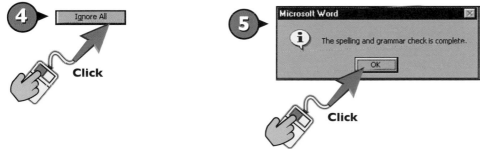

The Checker Is Not Perfect

Keep in mind that Word's spelling and grammar check isn't perfect itself—for example, it might think a slang word or sentence is an error. Fortunately, you can ignore Word's spelling and grammar suggestions. In addition, spell-check doesn't catch everything—you still need to proofread your documents.

4 ▶ Click the **Ignore All** button if Word finds a proper name.

5 ▶ Choose **OK** when Word displays a message telling you the spelling and grammar check is complete. This means all inaccuracies have been reviewed.

Task 20: Using the Thesaurus

Choosing Synonyms

Word's Thesaurus is a convenient tool that helps you replace words with more suitable ones. For example, if you find yourself using the same word too often, you can substitute another word so that your text doesn't sound redundant.

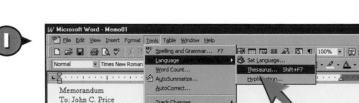

Start Here

Original Word

Click

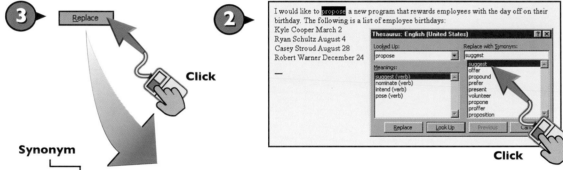

3 Replace

Click

Synonym

2

Click

I would like to suggest a new program that rewards employees with the day off on their birthday. The following is a list of employee birthdays:
Kyle Cooper March 2
Ryan Schultz August 4
Casey Stroud August 28
Robert Warner December 24

✓ **Word Meaning**
You can select the specific word meaning in the Meanings list box. This is convenient when you want to distinguish between nouns and verbs, for example.

1 Choose **Tools, Language, Thesaurus** to look up the word nearest the cursor.

2 In the **Replace with Synonym** list box, click the synonym you like for the word in the Looked Up list box.

3 Choose **Replace** to insert the new word.

End Task

Task 21: Tracking Changes

Start Here

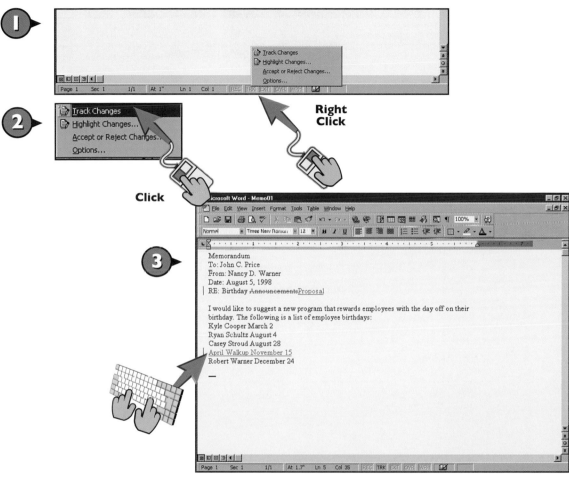

1

2

Track Changes
Highlight Changes...
Accept or Reject Changes...
Options...

Right Click

Track Changes
Highlight Changes...
Accept or Reject Changes...
Options...

Click

3

Microsoft Word - Memo01

File Edit View Insert Format Tools Table Window Help

Normal   Times New Roman   12

Memorandum
To: John C. Price
From: Nancy D. Warner
Date: August 5, 1998
RE: Birthday ~~Announcements~~ Proposal

I would like to suggest a new program that rewards employees with the day off on their
birthday. The following is a list of employee birthdays:
Kyle Cooper March 2
Ryan Schultz August 4
Casey Stroud August 28
April Walkup November 15
Robert Warner December 24

Page 1   Sec 1   1/1   At 1.7"   Ln 5   Col 35   REC TRK EXT OVR WPH

Collaborating and Correcting

Sometimes you find that you have to make corrections in a document, or perhaps you are working on a report in a team environment. To determine who made what changes when, you can track the changes onscreen with revision marks.

✓ **Turning Off Revisions**
You can quickly turn off revision marks by double-clicking **TRK** on the status bar.

✓ **Revision Names**
When you place the mouse pointer over a revision mark, the assigned name of the person who made the edit displays in a ScreenTip.

1 ▶ Right-click the grayed-out **TRK** on the status bar.

2 ▶ Choose **Track Changes** from the shortcut menu.

3 ▶ Type some changes into the document. The new text appears as a different color and underlined. Any changes to a line are flagged by a vertical black bar in the margin.

End Task

Task 22: Accepting or Rejecting Changes

The Joys of Being Edited

When you are ready to finalize any tracked changes in a document, you need to determine which changes you want to accept or reject. If you accept a change, the text change is made and the revision marks go away.

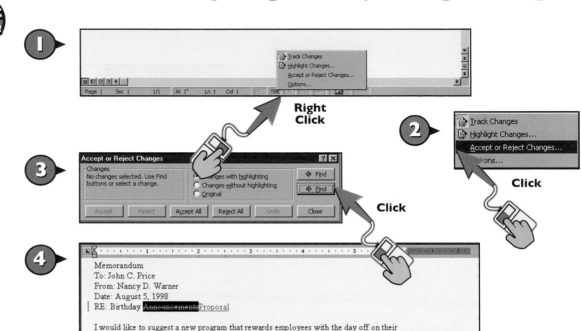

Right
Click

Click

Click

Click

Start Here

Finding Changes

If you want to skip over a change and review other changes, you can click the **Find** button to skip to the next revision. If you want to review a change earlier in the document, you can click the **Find** button to return to a previous change.

Click

1 ▶ Right-click **TRK** on the status bar.

2 ▶ Choose **Accept or Reject Changes** from the shortcut menu.

3 ▶ Choose **Find** in the Accept or Reject Changes dialog box. Word searches for, finds, and highlights the first (if any) occurrence of a tracked change.

4 ▶ Click the **Accept** button twice to accept the deleted word and add the new word. Word immediately takes you to the next tracked change.

Next Step

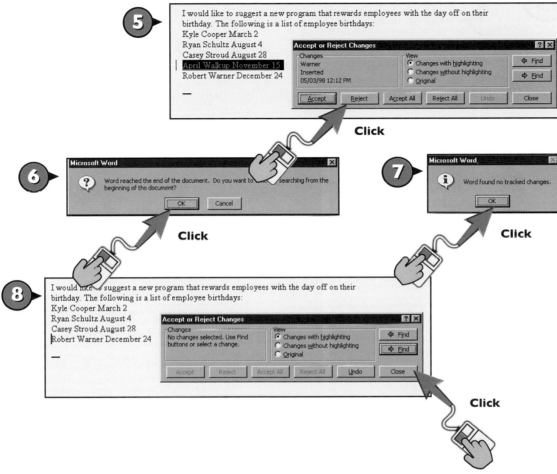

Click

Click

Click

Click

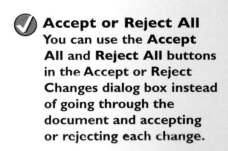

✅ **Accept or Reject All**
You can use the **Accept All** and **Reject All** buttons in the Accept or Reject Changes dialog box instead of going through the document and accepting or rejecting each change.

✅ **Skipping and Rejecting Changes**
If you don't want to accept a change, but you do want to leave the revision mark, you can choose to find the next revision mark. If you reject a change, Word returns to the original text, deleting the tracked change and removing the revision mark.

5 ▶ Click the **Reject** button to reject the next change. Word immediately takes you to the next tracked change.

6 ▶ Choose **OK** to continue checking from the beginning of the document.

7 ▶ Choose **OK** to acknowledge that Word found no more changes.

8 ▶ Choose **Close** to close the Accept or Reject Changes dialog box.

End Task

Page
37

PART 3

Working with Word Documents

You can format your documents with Word's formatting tools to make them more attractive and readable.

In addition to applying formatting to your documents, you can insert symbols, graphics, and page information (such as headers and footers).

After you have worked with your document and have it in the format you like, you can preview and print your document to see how it actually looks.

Tasks

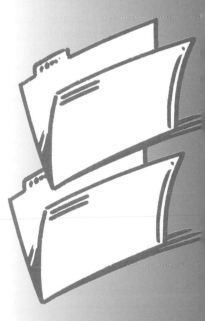

Using Basic Formatting Tools

To draw attention to important text in a document, you can make the text any combination of bold, italic, and underline. For example, perhaps you want to italicize the title of a book or emphasize the word "don't" by making it bold. In this task, you apply all three formatting options to the same text. You can apply these options individually as well.

✓ **Removing Formatting**
If you decide you don't want certain text to be bold, italic, or underline, you can select the text and click the appropriate button on the Formatting toolbar again. Notice that the button looks as if it has been pressed and then unpressed. Clicking the button turns the formatting option on and off.

Task 1: Applying Bold, Italic, and Underline

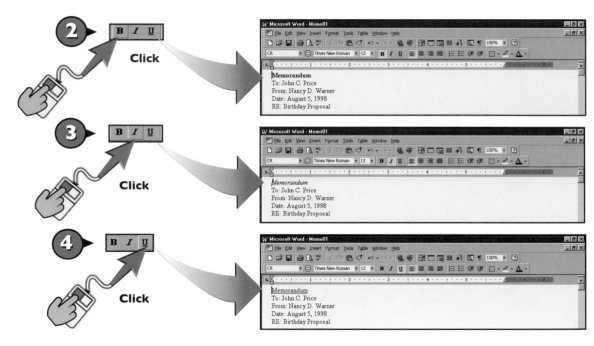

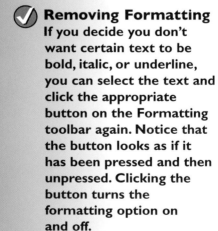

Start Here

Select the text you want to format. Part 2, Task 12 told you how.

Click the **Bold** button on the Formatting toolbar.

Click the **Italic** button on the Formatting toolbar.

Click the **Underline** button on the Formatting toolbar.

End Task

Task 2: Changing the Text Font

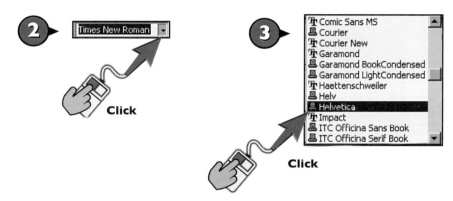

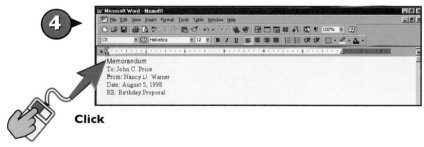

Using a Different Typeface

To draw attention to important words and phrases in a document, you can change the *font*. You might change a document title, for example, to make the title stand out at the top of the document.

1 Select the text you want to format. Part 2, Task 12 told you how.

2 Click the **Font** drop-down arrow on the Formatting toolbar.

3 Click the font (**Helvetica**) from the drop-down list box.

4 Click anywhere in the document to deselect the text.

 Change the Document Font
To change the font that appears as you type, choose it from the Font drop-down list and start typing. Your new text will be in the font you chose.

Task 3: Changing the Text Font Size

Making Text Bigger and Smaller

Sometimes you want text to unmistakably stand out in a document. One way to do this is to increase the text's size. If you make a word large, it stands a pretty good chance of being read. On the other hand, you might want to make text smaller so you can fit more information on a page.

Click

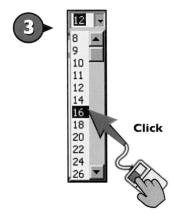

Click

Click

 Font Size Variations
The font sizes can vary, depending on the type of printer you have and the selected font. For example, the only printable font-size options for the Courier font are 10 and 12.

 Select the text you want to format. Part 2, Task 12 told you how.

 Click the **Font Size** drop-down arrow on the Formatting toolbar.

 Choose **16** from the **Font Size** drop-down list.

 Click anywhere in the document to deselect the text.

Task 4: Applying the Text Color

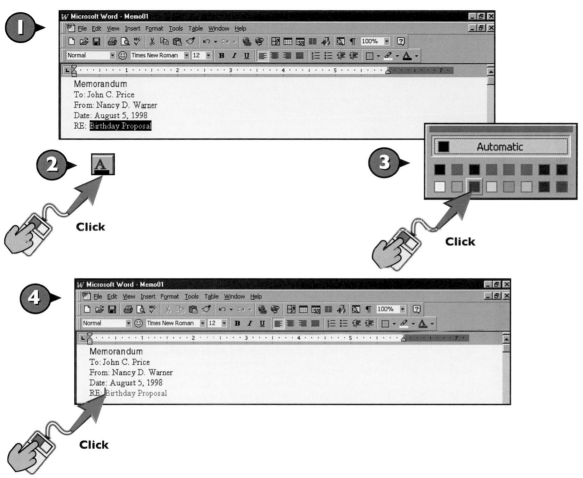

①

② 🅰 Click

③ Automatic Click

④ Click

Applying Text Font Color

Colors can quickly emphasize items in documents. For example, if you are creating a report to show an expense, you might want it to be in red. Or, if you want to compare information in two different plans—Plan A versus Plan B—applying two different colors can help distinguish your information.

① Select the text you want to format. Part 2, Task 12 told you how.

② Click the **Font Color** drop-down arrow on the Formatting toolbar. The Font Color selection box appears.

③ Click the red square.

④ Click anywhere in the document to deselect the text.

✅ **Changing Colors**
If you decide you want to change the text color to something else, repeat this task's steps and select a new color.

Task 5: Highlighting Text

Adding a Highlight to Text

When you want to draw attention to important text, highlight it. Highlighting is different from setting text color because you are altering the color of the text's background, not the text itself. Keep in mind that highlight colors print as shades of gray unless you use a color printer.

Start Here

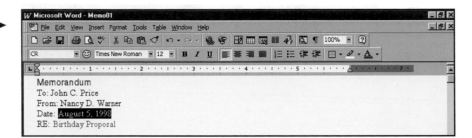

Click

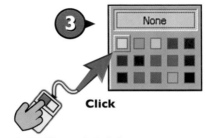
None
Click

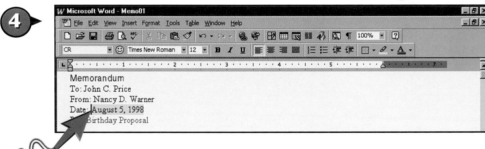
Click

✓ Highlighting Display Options

You can display or hide highlighting on the screen and in the printed document by choosing **Tools, Options.** Then choose the **View** tab and clear the **Highlight** check box.

Select the text you want to format. Part 2, Task 12 told you how.

Click the **Highlight** drop-down arrow on the Formatting toolbar. The Highlight Color selection box appears.

Click the yellow square.

Click anywhere in the document to deselect the text.

End Task

Task 6: Adding a Border to Text

Start Here

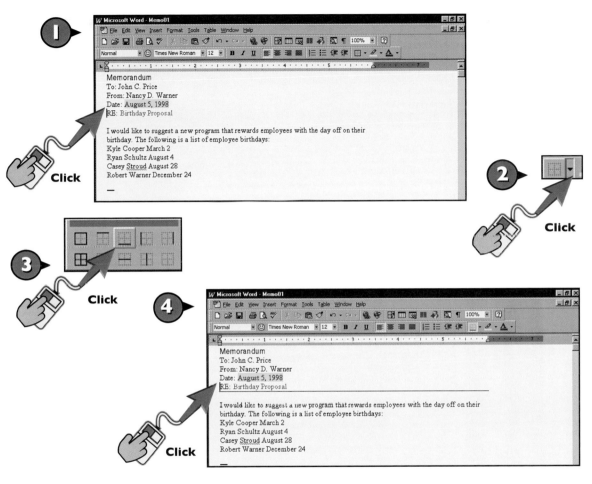

Adding a Border to Text

You add a border to any or all sides of a paragraph or selected text in Word. You can also add borders to tables, but we will cover that in Part 4, "Word 97 Tables." Borders can accentuate portions of your text, add a clean frame to your entire document, or divide sections of a document.

---

1 ▸ Click the line of a paragraph in your document where you want to add a border.

2 ▸ Click the **Border** drop-down arrow on the Formatting toolbar.

3 ▸ Choose the type of border you want to apply to the document. The border appears on the document.

4 ▸ Click anywhere in the document to deselect the text.

✓ More Border Options
For more border options, choose **Format, Borders** and **Shading** and then click the **Page Border** tab.

End Task

Task 7: Inserting Symbols

Using Symbol Characters

The **Symbol** command enables you to insert special characters, international characters, and symbols such as the registered trademark (®) and trademark (™) symbols. You can easily add these and other special characters to your Word documents.

Start Here

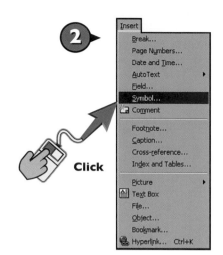

Click

Click

Close

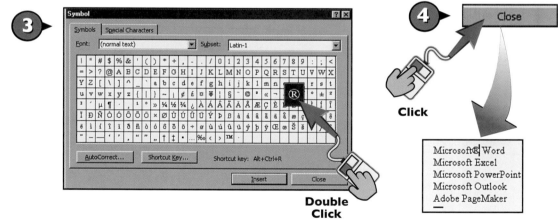

Click

Double Click

Microsoft® Word
Microsoft Excel
Microsoft PowerPoint
Microsoft Outlook
Adobe PageMaker

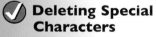 **Deleting Special Characters**
You can delete symbols and special characters just as you delete any other text—use the **Backspace** or **Delete** key.

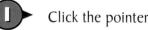 Click the pointer in the text where you want to add the symbol.

 Open the **Insert** menu and choose the **Symbol** option.

 In the Symbol dialog box, double-click the symbol you want to insert into your document.

 Choose **Close** to close the Symbol dialog box.

End Task

Task 8: Adding Numbers and Bullets

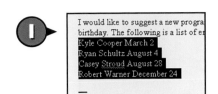

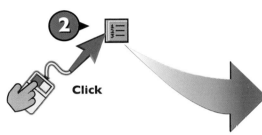

Click

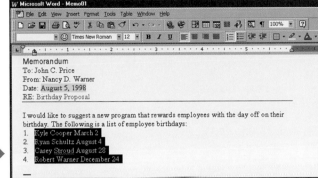

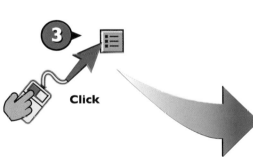

Click

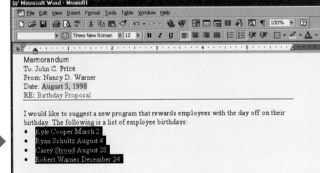

Working with Lists

With numbered and bulleted lists, you can present a series of information that helps readers visually follow a document's path. Numbered lists are useful for presenting a set of items or steps that must be in a particular order. Bulleted lists are useful for presenting a series of items when order doesn't matter.

✓ Creating a New List

If you haven't yet created the list you want to number or bullet, select the **Numbering** or **Bullets** button from the **Formatting toolbar** and then start typing the information. When you press **Enter** to start a new line, Word adds the number or bullet automatically. To stop adding bullets or numbers, press the **Enter** key more than once.

---

1 Select the text you want to format. Part 2, Task 12 told you how.

2 Click the **Numbering** button on the Formatting toolbar to create a numbered list.

3 Click the **Bullets** button on the Formatting toolbar if you prefer to have bullets.

End Task

Changing Alignment

When you enter text into a document, the text automatically aligns flush (even) with the left margin. However, you can change the alignment of text at any time. You can center it, make it flush with the right margin, or justify it (make it flush with both margins).

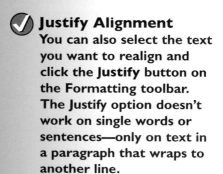

Justify Alignment
You can also select the text you want to realign and click the **Justify** button on the Formatting toolbar. The Justify option doesn't work on single words or sentences—only on text in a paragraph that wraps to another line.

Task 9: Changing Alignment

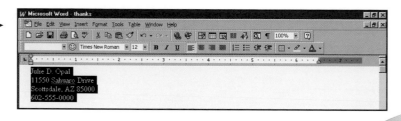

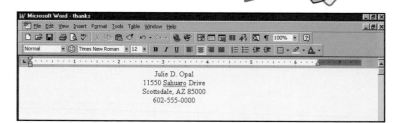

Click

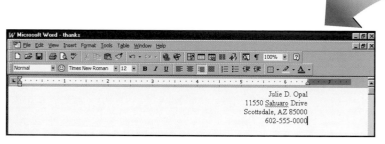

Click

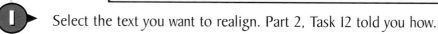

1. ▶ Select the text you want to realign. Part 2, Task 12 told you how.

2. ▶ Click the **Center** button on the Formatting toolbar.

3. ▶ Click the **Align Right** button on the Formatting toolbar.

Task 10: Indenting Paragraphs

Start Here

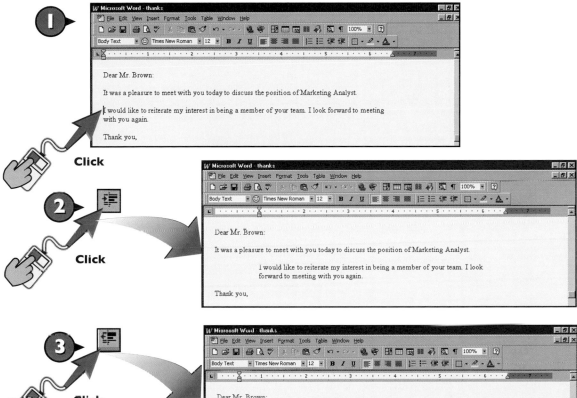

Click

Click

Click

Formatting with Indents

You can indent an entire paragraph to the right of the left margin to make it stand out. For example, if you are creating a contract, you might want to indent certain paragraphs to make them subordinate to other text.

✓ Hanging Indents

When you're creating a résumé, you might find it convenient to use the hanging indent. With a hanging indent, all but the first line of a paragraph is moved to the right, giving a clean presentation of information with the emphasis on the first line. To select a hanging indent, click the paragraph and choose **Format, Paragraph**. In the Paragraph dialog box, click on the **Indents and Spacing** tab and choose **Hanging** from the **Special** drop-down list.

1. ▶ Click somewhere in the paragraph you want to indent.

2. ▶ Click the **Increase Indent** button on the Formatting toolbar twice. The indent moves to the right two tab spaces.

3. ▶ Click the **Decrease Indent** button on the Formatting toolbar once. The indent moves to the left one tab space.

Task 11: Setting Tabs with the Ruler

Creating Tab Stops

You can set different types of tab stops: left (default), right, decimal, or center tabs. Setting tabs is useful for indenting paragraphs at one or more tab stops.

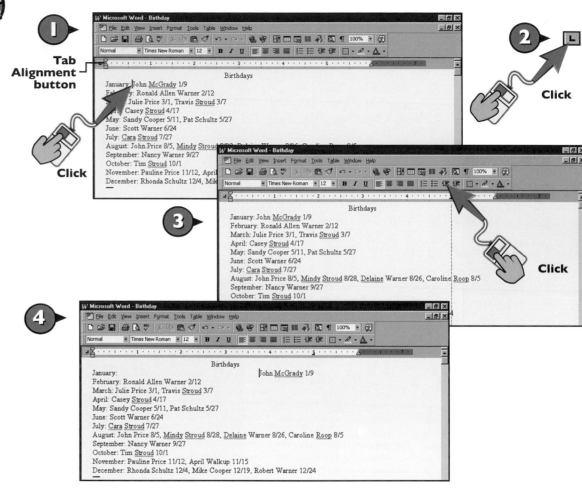

✓ **Tab Options**

An "L" is a Left tab, an upside down "T" is a Center tab, a backward "L" is a Right tab, and an upside down "T" with a dot is a Decimal tab. You cycle through the tab options each time you click the Tab Alignment button.

✓ **Removing a Tab**

If you want to remove a tab stop, select the text for which you set the tab, point to the tab marker, left-click and drag it off the ruler, and then release the mouse button. The tab stop disappears.

1 ▸ Click in the paragraph where you want to set a tab.

2 ▸ Click the **Tab Alignment** button (see the Tab Option tip) to choose the type of tab stop you want.

3 ▸ Move the mouse pointer to the place on the ruler where you want the tab stop, and click once.

4 ▸ Press the **Tab** key to align the text with the tab stop.

Task 12: Changing Line Spacing

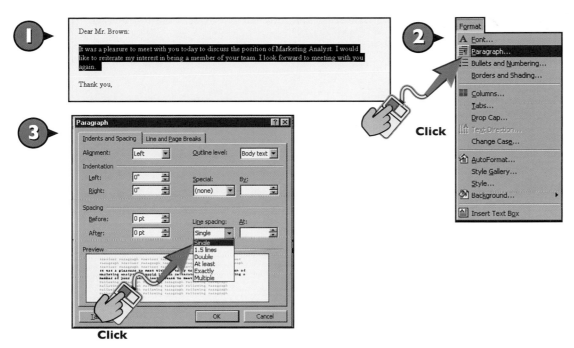

Click

Click

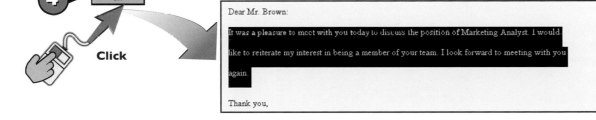

OK

Click

Select the text you want to alter. Part 2, Task 12 told you how.

1 Select the text you want to alter. Part 2, Task 12 told you how.

2 Choose **Format, Paragraph**. The Paragraph dialog box opens.

3 In the **Line spacing** drop-down list, choose the spacing you desire.

4 Choose **OK**.

Adding Space Between Lines

Have you ever found yourself in a situation where you needed to fill up a page with text but you just couldn't think of any more text to write? Line spacing can be a handy tool that can increase (or decrease, if needed) the amount of vertical space between lines of text—so you can stretch one-and-a-half pages to fill two pages. Word uses single-line spacing by default.

✓ **Spacing Above and Below**
You can also alter the amount of space above or below your line of text by altering the Above and Below options in the Paragraph dialog box.

Task 13: Inserting a Section Break

Dividing Documents into Sections

Section breaks enable you to format each section separately; for example, different portions of your document can have different margins. Word has four kinds of section breaks: **Next Page**, which starts the new section on a new page; **Continuous**, which starts the new section on the current page; **Odd Page**, which starts the new section on the next odd-numbered page; and **Even Page**, which starts the new section on the next even-numbered page.

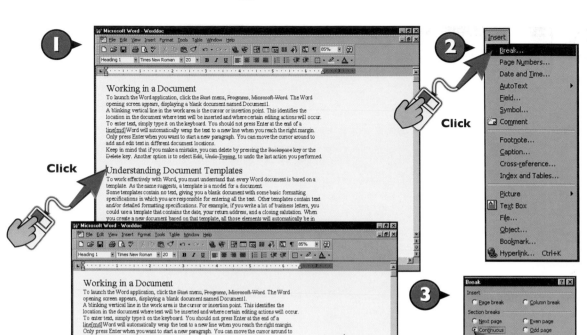

Start Here

Click

Click

Section Break

Click

Click

Click

✓ **Viewing Section Breaks**

Notice that section-break double-dotted lines display only in the Normal and Outline views. See Part 2, Task 10, to review how to change views.

1 Click the pointer where you want to insert a section break.

2 Choose **Insert, Break**.

3 In the Break dialog box, choose the type of section break you would like to insert (for example, **Continuous**).

4 Choose **OK**. The section break appears in the document.

End Task

Task 14: Inserting a Page Break

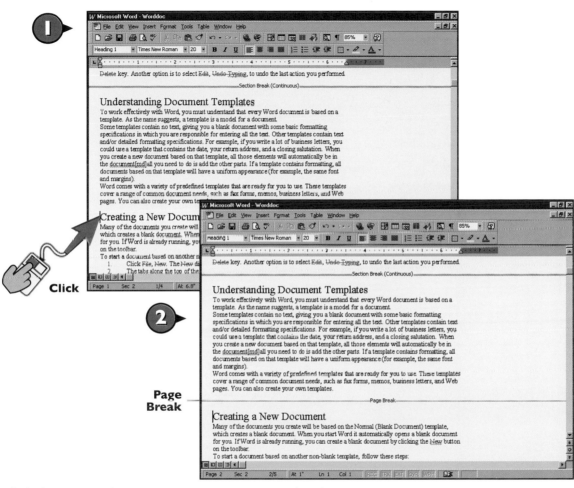

Click

Page Break

Forcing Text to the Next Page

A page break is the point where one page ends and another page begins. When a page is filled with text, Word automatically begins a new page by inserting a page break for you; however, there are times when you want to manually insert a page break. For example, if you are writing a report with multiple topic sections, you might want each topic to begin at the top of a new page.

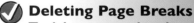

Deleting Page Breaks
To delete a page break, simply select the manual page break (by clicking the mouse pointer once on the page break's dotted line in Normal view) and press the **Delete** key. To change to Normal view, refer to Part 2, Task 10.

1 ▶ Click the cursor where you want to insert a page break.

2 ▶ Press the **Ctrl+Enter** keys simultaneously to insert the page break in your document.

End Task

Task 15: Adding Columns

Creating Newsletter Layouts

You can display text in multiple columns on a page in a Word document. This is convenient when you want to create a brochure or newsletter. Keep in mind that you must be in **Page Layout** view to work with columns in your document. See Part 2, Task 10 for instructions about changing views.

✓ **Adding Columns to Selected Text**
You can make only a portion of a document into columns by selecting the specific text and then adding the columns.

✓ **Columns in the Ruler**
You can tell that the columns have been added to a document by looking at the top ruler. Column separators appear where the columns are divided.

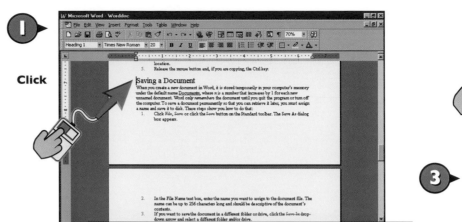

Start Here

Click

Click

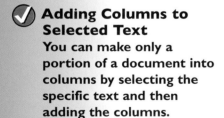

Click

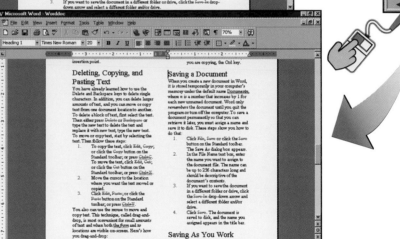

1 Click the cursor where you want to insert columns.

2 Click the **Columns** button on the Standard toolbar.

3 Move the mouse pointer over the number of columns you want and click the number of columns.

End Task

Task 16: Inserting Graphics

Start Here

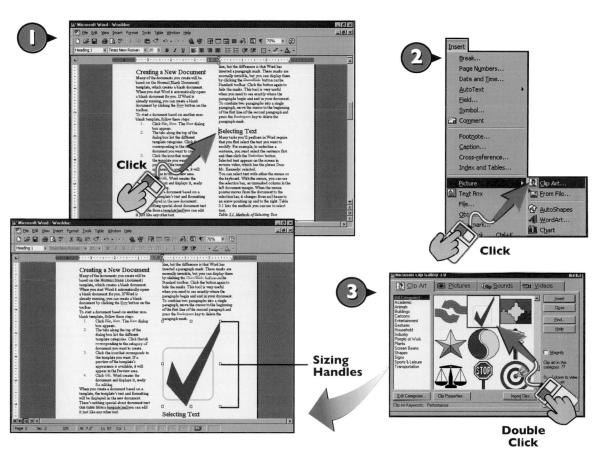

Click

Click

Sizing Handles

Double Click

Adding Pictures to Documents

Clip art adds visual interest to your Word documents. With the Microsoft **Clip Gallery**, you can choose from more than 1,000 professionally prepared images.

1 Click the cursor where you want the clip art to appear.

2 Choose **Insert, Picture, Clip Art**. You might see a message telling you that additional pieces of clip art are on the Office 97 CD-ROM.

3 Double-click on the piece of clip art you want (you can scroll through the Microsoft Clip Gallery 3.0 dialog box options), which will insert the clip art into your document.

✓ **Picture Toolbar**
When you select a picture, the Picture toolbar appears with tools you can use to crop the picture, add a border to it, or adjust its brightness and contrast. If the Picture toolbar doesn't appear, right-click the picture and then click **Show Picture Toolbar** on the shortcut menu.

End Task

Task 17: Inserting Page Numbers

Numbering Pages

Word can automatically insert page numbers in your documents and print the page numbers in the position you specify. That way, you don't have to manually enter and manage the page numbers.

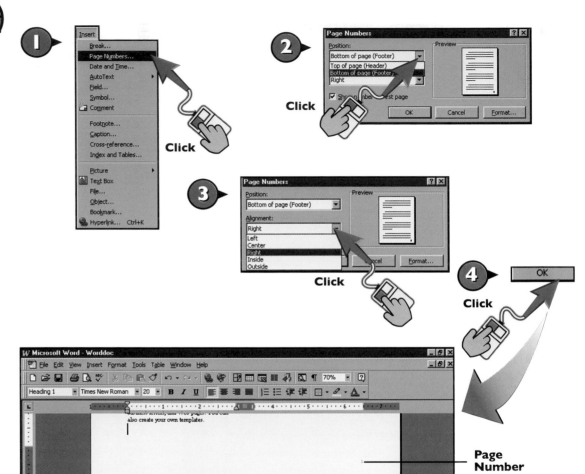

Start Here

Click

Click

Click

Click

Page Number

✓ Show Number on First Page
If you don't want a page number on the first page, click to remove the check mark from the **Show Number on First Page** check box of the Page Numbers dialog box.

1 ▶ Choose **Insert, Page Numbers**.

2 ▶ In the Page Numbers dialog box, click the **Position** drop-down arrow to select whether you want the page number at the top or bottom of the page.

3 ▶ Click the **Alignment** drop-down arrow to select whether you want the page number at the left, center, or right side of the page or on the inside or outside of the page.

4 ▶ Choose **OK**. You can see the page number (grayed out) in Page Layout view.

End Task

Task 18: Inserting Footnotes and Endnotes

Start Here

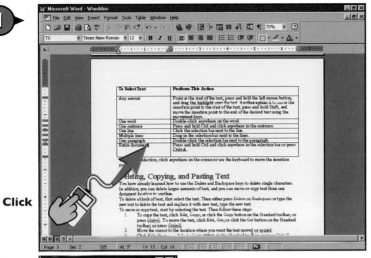

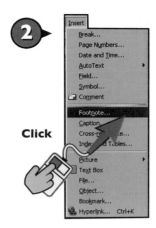

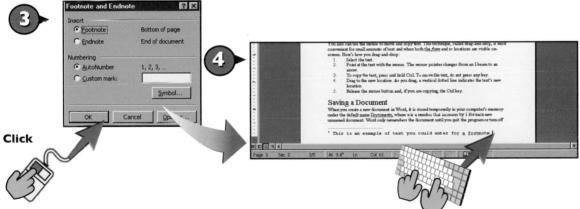

Adding Footnotes

Footnotes can be used to add comments and references in a document. You might use a footnote at the end of a page to tell the reader what the source of your information was. A footnote consists of the note reference mark and the corresponding note text, which are linked.

✓ **Viewing Footnotes**
If you want to view your footnotes, place the mouse pointer on the note reference mark in the document. The text you typed appears above the reference mark.

✓ **Endnotes**
If you want to insert an endnote instead, click the Endnote option on the Footnote and Endnote dialog box. You might use endnotes to cite references you researched for a paper.

1 ▶ Click the cursor where you want to insert a footnote.

2 ▶ Choose **Insert, Footnote**.

3 ▶ Choose **OK** in the Footnote and Endnote dialog box to accept the default options of inserting a footnote with AutoNumber.

4 ▶ Type the text you want to appear in the footnote. Word automatically places the cursor at the end of the page and numbers the footnote.

End Task

Working with Headers and Footers

Headers and footers are text that prints at the top and bottom of every page in a document—headers at the top, footers at the bottom. For example, you might want to place your name and the date at the top of the document and the document's name at the bottom. You can include text, page numbers, or the current date and time, and you can even apply formatting to the information in a header and footer.

✓ **Moving in Headers and Footers**
Press the **Tab** key to move from left-aligning to center-aligning to right-aligning the header or footer.

Task 19: Inserting a Header and Footer

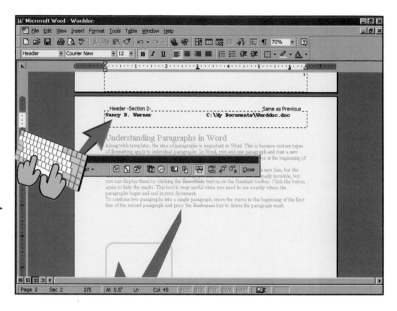

Click

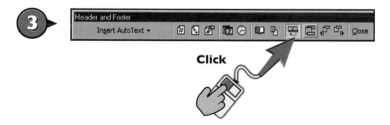

Click

Choose **View, Header and Footer** to open the Header and Footer toolbar. Word automatically places the cursor in the Header area.

Type the text you want to print at the top of each page.

Click the **Switch Between Header and Footer** button to go from the header to the footer.

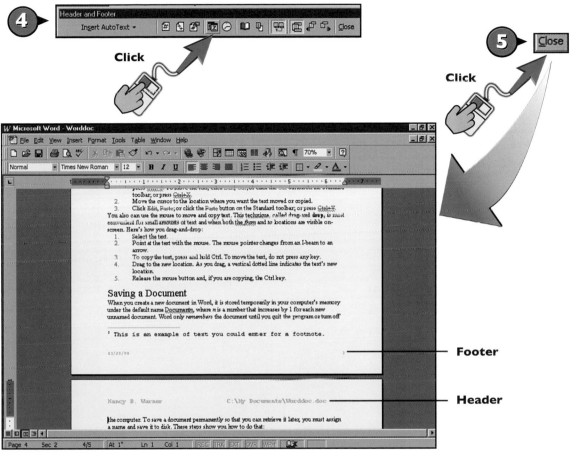

Click

Click

Footer

Header

4 ▶ Click the **Insert Date** button to add the date to the footer.

5 ▶ Click the **Close Header and Footer** button to return to the main document.

✓ **Switching Between Header and Footer**
You can click the Switch Between Header and Footer button on the Header and Footer toolbar as many times as you need to review your edits.

Task 20: Setting Page Margins

Adjusting Margins

You can adjust the top, bottom, left, and right margins for a single page or for your entire document. For example, you might need to fit a large amount of text on one page, on which you need to increase the margins for the document's printable area. Word's default margins are 1 inch for the top and bottom and 1.25 inches for the left and right.

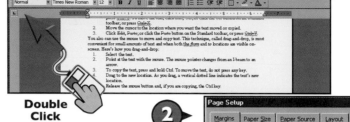

Double Click

1.5 Margin

Click

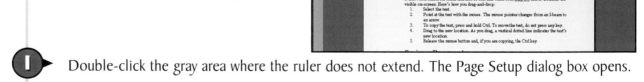

✓ Portrait and Landscape

If you need to alter your page from Portrait to Landscape or increase the size of your document (for example, to legal size—8.5 by 14 inches), modify the **Paper Size** tab on the **Page Setup** dialog box.

1 ▶ Double-click the gray area where the ruler does not extend. The Page Setup dialog box opens.

2 ▶ Type the new margin settings (for example, Left **1.5** and Right **1.5**).

3 ▶ Choose **OK**. You can view the new page margins applied in the document by looking at the new locations of the indent markers on the ruler.

End Task

Task 21: Previewing a Document

Start Here

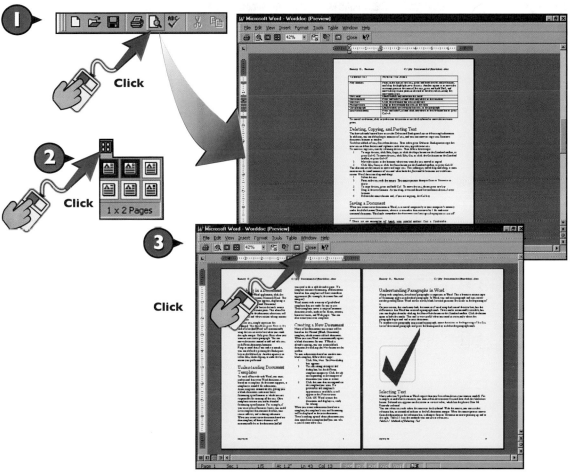

Click

Click

1 x 2 Pages

Click

Seeing What Your Document Will Look Like Printed

Print Preview enables you to see document pages onscreen as they will appear printed on paper, displaying page numbers, headers, footers, fonts, font sizes and styles, orientation, and margins. Previewing your document is a great way to catch formatting errors such as incorrect margins. You will save costly printer paper and time by previewing your documents before you print.

1 Click the **Print Preview** button on the Standard toolbar. You can press the **page-up** and **page-down** keys to navigate through each page of your document.

2 Click the **Multiple Pages** button on the Print Preview toolbar and click the number of pages you want to view at a time.

3 Click the **Close** button on the Print Preview toolbar to return to the document.

Viewing Pages
If you are viewing multiple pages, you can click the **One Page** button on the Print Preview toolbar to return to viewing one page at a time.

End Task

Task 22: Zooming a Previewed Document

Getting a Closer Look at Your Text

If you want to zoom in and get a closer look at text in your document while you are previewing it, you can select a higher percentage of magnification. On the other hand, if you want to zoom out so more of the page—or even the whole document—shows on the screen at one glance, select a lower percentage of magnification.

✓ Zoom Control

The Zoom Control box displays the percentage by which you are magnifying the document. When zooming in on a document, the mouse pointer becomes a magnifying glass with a minus sign (–). When zooming out of a document, the mouse pointer becomes a magnifying glass with a plus sign (+).

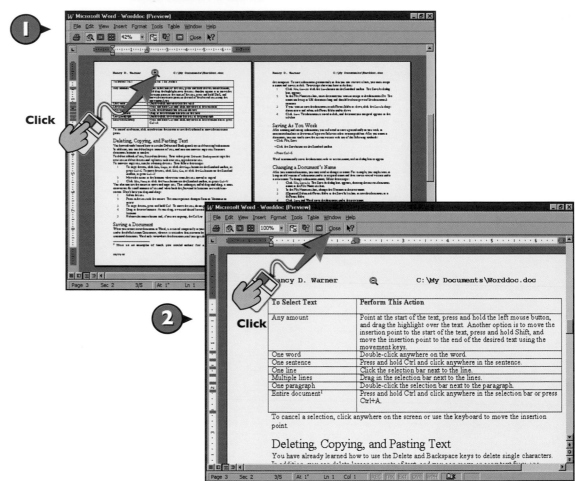

Click

Click

1 Preview the document by using the steps in Task 21. Then click once directly on the document to magnify the text to 100 percent.

2 Choose **Close** to exit Print Preview.

Task 23: Printing a Document

Start Here

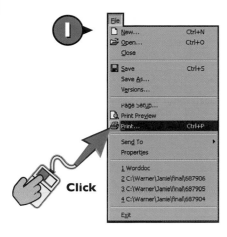

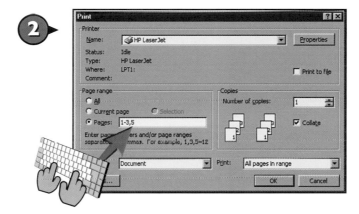

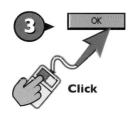

Click

OK

Click

Putting Words to Paper

Word makes it easy to print a document and enables you to select the printer and font settings. You can print the entire document, a single page, specific page ranges, specific separate pages, or selected text. You can also specify the number of copies to print and collate the copies as you print.

✓ **Automatically Print Defaults**
You can just click the **Print** button on the Standard toolbar. Word prints the document, using its default settings and skipping the Print dialog box.

✓ **Canceling a Print Job**
You can tell Word is printing the document because of the **Printing** icon on the status bar. Double-click the **Printing** icon on the status bar to immediately cancel a print job.

---

1 ▶ Choose **File, Print**.

2 ▶ From the **Print** dialog box, select printing options (for example, you can choose to print pages **1-3,5**).

3 ▶ Choose **OK**. The document pages print.

End Task

PART 4

Word 97 Tables

When you are working in a document, you might find you want to organize your data and perform some simple calculations. This would be a good time to add a Word table. If you want to do more advanced calculations, you should use Microsoft Excel (see Part 6 "Working with Formulas and Functions").

In a table, you can organize information in a row and column format. Each entry in a table, called a *cell*, is independent of all other entries. You can have almost any number of rows and columns in a table. You also have a great deal of control over the size and formatting of each cell.

Tasks

Task 1: Creating a New Table

Making a Table

Instead of creating long lists of information and trying to cross-reference these lists (for example, a shopping list and a separate, corresponding price list), you can simply add a table to your document. You can use tables to organize information and create side-by-side columns of text for organizing and presenting data in an easy-to-read manner.

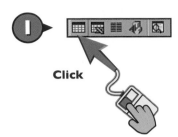

Click

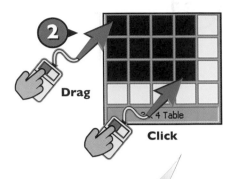

Drag

Click

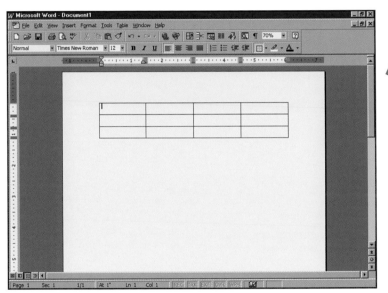

✓ Alter Margins Before You Begin

You will save a lot of time if you set your page margins before you insert a table. Otherwise, you have to select all the tables and alter the margins afterwards—which can be tricky. See Part 3, Task 20 for instructions on setting page margins.

 Click the **Insert Table** button on the Standard toolbar.

 Drag the mouse pointer over the grid to determine the number of columns and rows for the table, and click to select the size table you want. Word creates a table for you in the dimensions you selected.

Task 2: Entering Text into a Table

Start Here

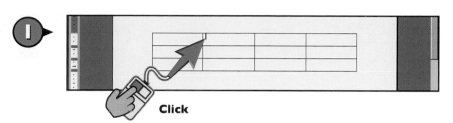

Click

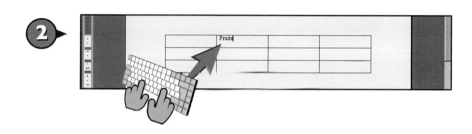

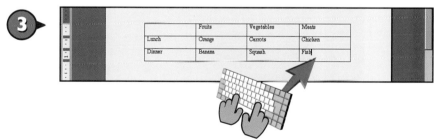

Typing Information into a Table

A table is of no use to you without data in it. Placing data in table format turns it into useful information—suddenly columns and rows represent organized lists of items.

1 Click the first table cell in which you would like to enter text.

2 Type your text.

3 Press either the **Tab** key or the arrow keys to move around the table; then type more text.

! WARNING
When you press **Enter** in a Word table, you don't move down a cell (as you do in Excel); you simply wrap to the next line within the cell. To move to a different cell, use the arrow keys.

Altering Row Height and Column Width

When you have text in your table, you might notice either too much or too little space between the table's lines and the text. Word enables you to easily change the row height and column width to minimize or maximize space.

Task 3: Altering Row Height and Column Width

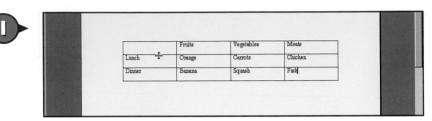

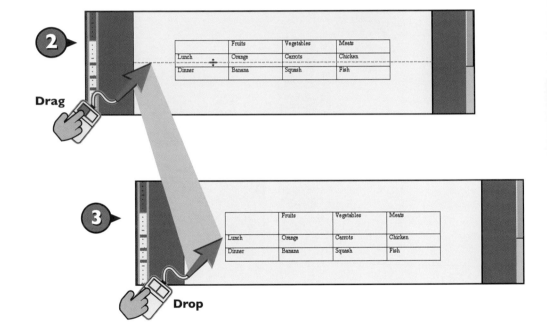

Drag

Drop

✓ **Formatting Tables**
After you add a Word table, you can format it with AutoFormat (see Task 6) or you can apply some of the same formatting you can add to an Excel worksheet (see Part 5, "Excel 97 Basics").

1 Move the mouse pointer over the bottom edge of the row you want to alter. The mouse pointer changes shape as the figure shows.

2 Press and hold down the left mouse button and drag the row edge to the new size.

3 Release the mouse button to drop the line in the new location.

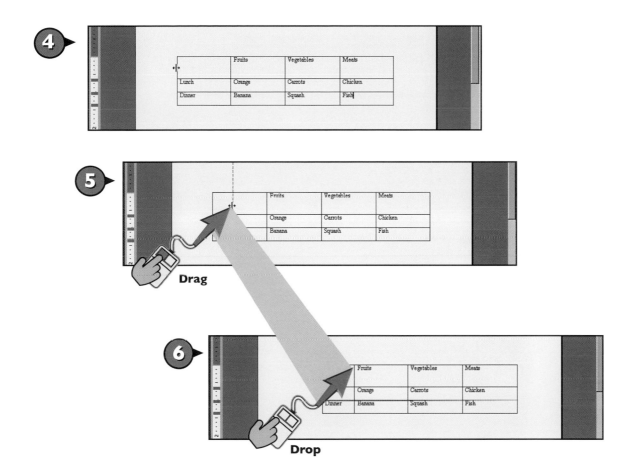

Drag

Drop

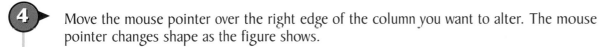

4 ▸ Move the mouse pointer over the right edge of the column you want to alter. The mouse pointer changes shape as the figure shows.

5 ▸ Press and hold down the left mouse button and drag the column edge to the new size.

6 ▸ Release the mouse button to drop the line in the new location.

✓ Page Layout View
Notice that the ruler is visible on the left side of the screen in this task's figures. That's because Word is in Page Layout view. See Part 2, Task 10, to learn how to change to Page Layout view.

End Task

Adding Rows and Columns

When working with Word tables, you might find you need another row or column after you have already created the table. Word makes it easy to add rows and columns while working in a table. Word always inserts a row above (and identical to) the row you select and a column to the left of (and identical to) the column you select.

✓ **Adding a Row at the End**

To add a row to the bottom of the table, you must place the cursor at the end of any text in the bottom right cell in the table and press the **Tab** key.

Task 4: Adding Table Rows and Columns

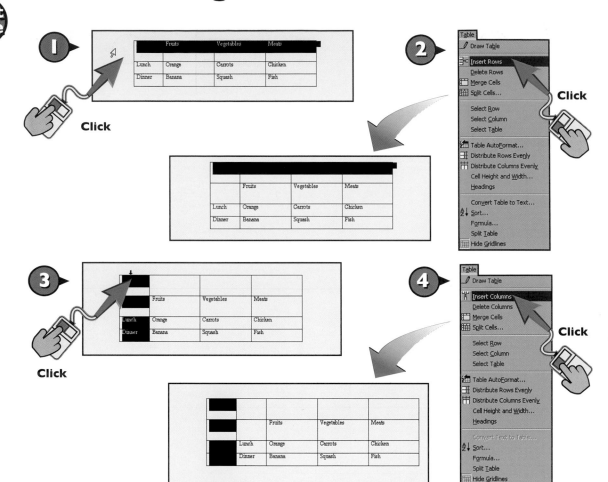

1 Click in the margin to the left of the row you would like to insert a row above; the row becomes highlighted. (Notice that the mouse pointer switched from pointing up-left to up-right.)

2 Choose **Table, Insert Rows**; the new row appears.

3 Move the mouse pointer over the column you want to alter. When the pointer turns into a downward arrow, click to select the column.

4 Choose **Table, Insert Columns**; the column appears.

Task 5: Deleting Table Rows and Columns

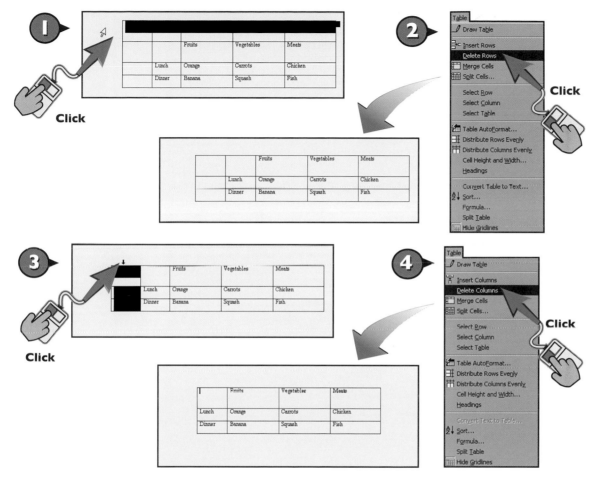

Removing Table Information

After you have been working with a table, you might determine that some of the information is not necessary. Word enables you to delete this information quickly and easily.

① Click in the margin to the left of the row you would like to delete. (Notice that the mouse pointer switched from pointing up-left to up-right.)

② Choose **Table, Delete Rows**; the row disappears.

③ Move the mouse pointer over the column you want to delete. When the pointer turns into a downward arrow, click to select the column.

④ Choose **Table, Delete Columns**; the column disappears.

 Deleting Text Only
Selecting a row or column and then pressing the **Delete** key removes the text within the cells and leaves empty rows and columns.

Task 6: AutoFormatting Tables

Automatically Formatting Tables

Tables present information in a way that can be quite effective to understand and review. To make a table look even better, you can add all types of formats to it. If you don't want to take the time to format the table on your own, Word can quickly format it for you.

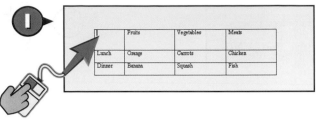

Click

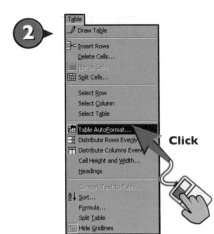

Click

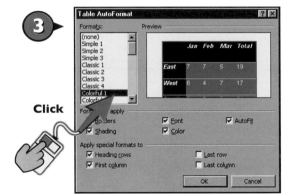

Click

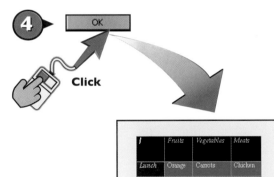

Click

✓ **No Table Format**
To quickly remove all formatting from a table, return to the Table AutoFormat dialog box, choose **(none)** from the **Formats** selection, and then choose OK.

1 ▶ Click in any cell of the table you want to format.

2 ▶ Choose **Table, Table AutoFormat**.

3 ▶ In the Table AutoFormat dialog box, click an option in the **Formats** list to view a format sample in the Preview area (for example, **Colorful 1**).

4 ▶ Choose **OK** to automatically apply the format to your table.

End Task

Task 7: Converting a Table to Text

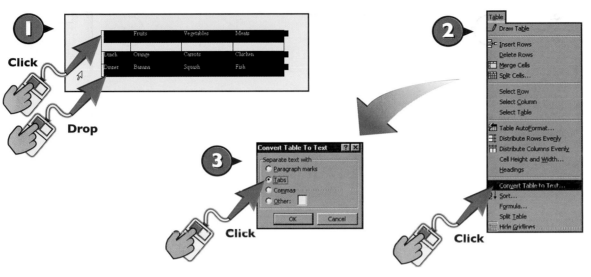

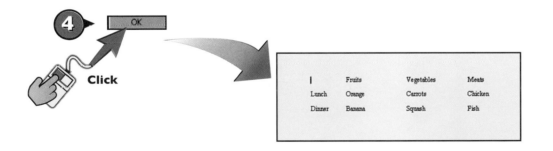

Making Text from a Table

Sometimes you might want to use the information in a table without all the formatting. For example, you can convert the table to text and save it as a file you can import into a database. When you convert a table to text, you can specify several ways (such as commas, tab characters, or paragraph marks) to separate the table's cells.

---

1 Click in the margin to the left of the first row of the table, and then drag the pointer to the last row of the table.

2 Choose **Table, Convert Table to Text**.

3 In the Convert Table to Text dialog box, choose how you want to separate the table's cells (for example, choose **Tabs**).

4 Choose **OK**. Word converts the selected table into tabbed columns.

 Text to a Table
You can also convert text to a table. Select the text you want to convert, right-click on the selected text, and click **Convert Text to a Table** from the shortcut menu.

Task 8: Deleting a Table

Removing a Table

You might decide not to use a table in your document after all. In this case, you will want to delete the entire table from your document.

Start Here

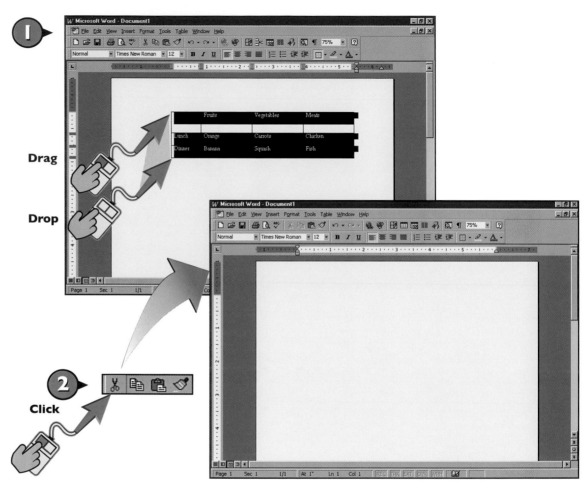

Drag

Drop

Click

Delete All Rows

Another way to delete the entire table is to select all the rows in the table and choose **Table, Delete Rows**.

 Click the margin to the left of the first row of the table, and then drag the pointer to the last row to select the table.

 Click the **Cut** button on the Standard toolbar; the table disappears.

End Task

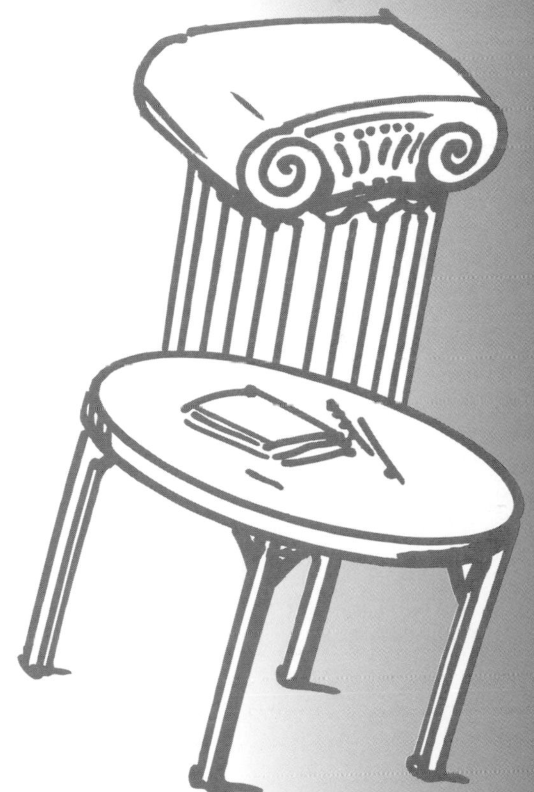

PART 5

Excel 97 Basics

When you start the program, Excel displays a blank workbook. A **workbook** is a file in which you store your data, similar to a three-ring binder. Within a workbook are worksheets, chart sheets, and macro sheets. A new workbook contains three sheets, named Sheet1 through Sheet3. You can add sheets, up to 255 total per workbook, depending on your computer's available memory.

Multiple sheets help you organize, manage, and consolidate your data. For example, you might want to create a sales forecast for the first quarter of the year. Sheet1, Sheet2, and Sheet3 could contain worksheet data for January, February, and March, Sheet4 a summary for the three months of sales data, and Sheet5 a chart showing sales over the three-month period.

A **worksheet** is a grid of **columns** and **rows**. The intersection of any column and row is called a **cell**. Each cell in a worksheet has a unique cell reference, the designation formed by combining the row and column headings. For example, A8 is the reference of the cell at the intersection of column A and row 8.

The cell pointer is a cross-shaped pointer that appears over cells in the worksheet. You use the cell pointer to select any cell in the worksheet. The selected cell is called the active cell. You always have at least one cell selected at all times.

A **range** is a specified group of cells. A range can be a single cell, a column, a row, or any combination of cells, columns, and rows. Range coordinates identify a range. The first element in the range coordinates is the location of the upper-left cell in the range; the second element is the location of the lower-right cell. A colon separates these two elements. The range A1:C3, for example, includes the cells A1, A2, A3, B1, B2, B3, C1, C2, and C3.

Tasks

Getting Started in Excel

Excel offers many features to help you manage numeric information more easily. You can use Excel to create worksheets, databases, charts, and macros. These aren't the only kinds of things you can create—the best way to find out what you can do is to get started working in Excel.

✅ **Starting Excel from a File**

Another way to start the Excel application is to double-click on an Excel file in an Explorer window. The application automatically launches and opens to the file you selected.

Task 1: Starting Excel

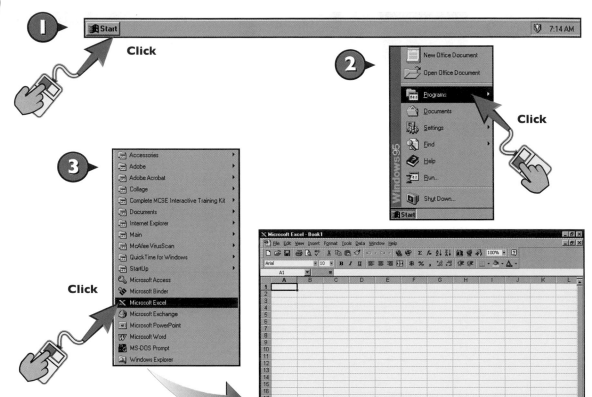

Click

Click

Click

Click the **Start** button on the taskbar.

Move the mouse pointer to **Programs**.

Choose the **Microsoft Excel** option.

End Task

Task 2: Entering Data

Start Here

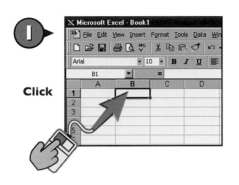

Click

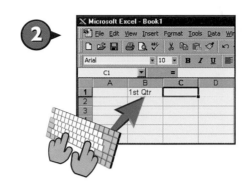

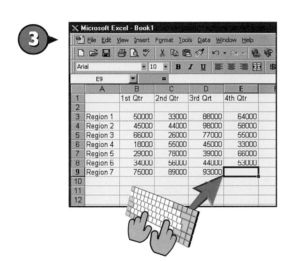

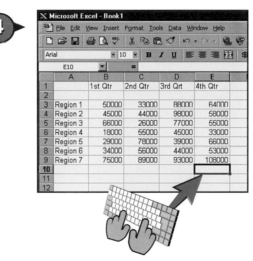

Typing Information into the Worksheet

The easiest way to enter data is to start typing when Excel opens a worksheet. You will notice that when you type numbers, they align by default to the right; when you type text, it aligns by default to the left. You will also notice that whatever you type appears in the Formula bar.

① Click the mouse button when the pointer (notice that it is a plus sign) is in the cell you want (for example, cell B1).

② Type text into a cell (in this case, **1st Qtr**) and press the right-arrow key to move one cell to the right.

③ Type data similar to the figure until you are familiar with how Excel displays the data in a worksheet.

④ Type your last cell of data and press **Enter**.

✓ Accepting Entered Data

When you have entered data into a cell, you can do one of two things to accept the data in the cell: Press the Enter key (which moves you to the next cell below) or press an arrow key (which moves you to a cell in that direction).

End Task

Task 3: Moving Around a Workbook

Getting Around in a Workbook

Each tab in a workbook represents a worksheet. To view a sheet, click its tab. You can keep data stored on different worksheets pertinent to an entire workbook. For example, you might want to keep sales data for the past two years. You can keep each year separately on its own worksheet but save everything in the same workbook file. You can also assign each worksheet a specific name and add more worksheets.

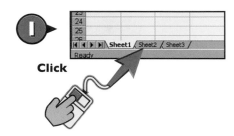

Click

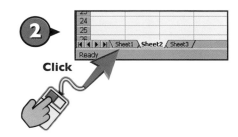

Click

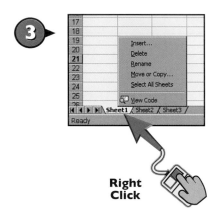

Right Click

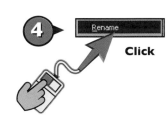

Click

✓ **Add a Worksheet**

You can add a worksheet as quickly as you can add a row or column (covered in Tasks 11 and 12). To add a worksheet, choose Insert, Worksheet. Excel places another worksheet to the left of the worksheet in which you are working.

1 ▶ Click the **Sheet2** tab at the bottom left of the worksheet.

2 ▶ Click the **Sheet1** tab to return to the worksheet where you entered data.

3 ▶ Right-click the **Sheet1** tab.

4 ▶ Choose **Rename** from the shortcut menu.

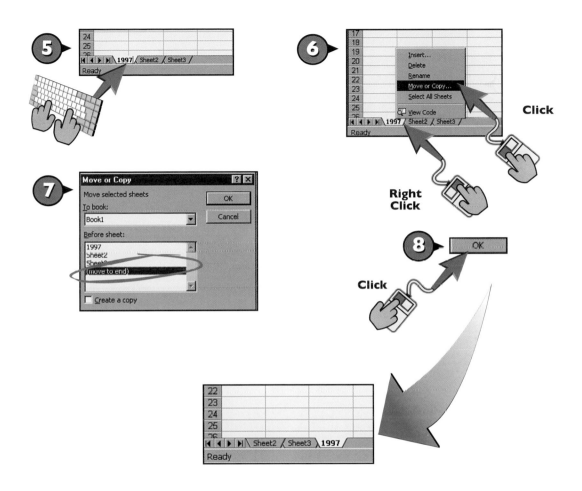

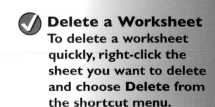

Click

5 ▶ Type the name you would like for the worksheet (for example, **1997**) and press **Enter**.

6 ▶ Right-click the **1997** tab and choose **Move or Copy** from the shortcut menu.

7 ▶ Choose the location you would like to move the worksheet to—for example, choose **(move to end)**—in the Move or Copy dialog box.

8 ▶ Choose **OK** to move the worksheet.

✅ **Delete a Worksheet**
To delete a worksheet quickly, right-click the sheet you want to delete and choose **Delete** from the shortcut menu.

Task 4: Moving Around a Worksheet

Getting Around in a Spreadsheet

Using a mouse is often the easiest way to move around the worksheet; you use the vertical or horizontal scroll-bars to see other portions of the worksheet. However, you can also use the keyboard to move around, and with Excel's Go To command, you can quickly jump to cells that are out of view.

Start Here

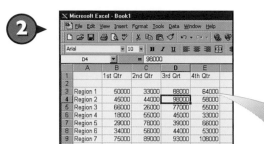

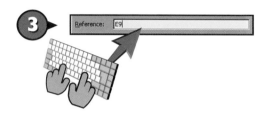

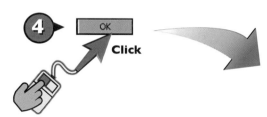

OK
Click

✓ **Beginning of the Worksheet**
Press the **Ctrl+A** keys simultaneously to move immediately to cell A1 at the top left of the worksheet.

1 ▶ Press the **arrow** keys to get the feel of how you can move from cell to cell.

2 ▶ Press the **Ctrl+G** keys simultaneously; the Go To dialog box appears.

3 ▶ Type the location of the cell you would like to go to in the Reference text box.

4 ▶ Choose **OK** to move immediately to the cell reference.

End Task

Task 5: Saving a Workbook

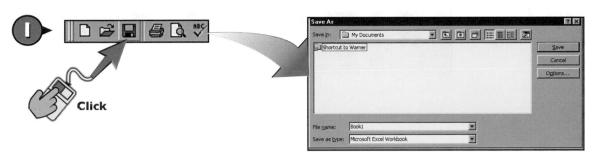

Click

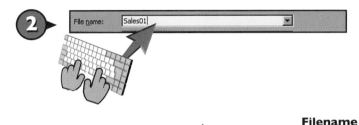

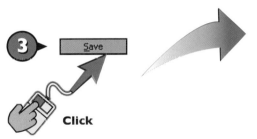

Filename

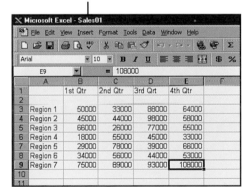

Click

Storing Your Work on Disk

Until you save the workbook you are working in, the data in the file is not stored on disk. It is good practice to regularly save your workbooks as you work in them. When you save a workbook, you can retrieve it later to work on.

✔ **Save In Option**
If you don't want to save your file in the My Documents directory, you can select the **Save in** drop-down list box and maneuver through your folders to save the file in a different location.

✔ **Save Button**
If you have already named the file, you can click on the **Save** button on the Standard toolbar to quickly save your recent changes.

1 ▶ Click the **Save** button on the Standard toolbar.

2 ▶ Type a different filename if you want (for example, **Sales01**) in the Save As dialog box.

3 ▶ Choose **Save** in the Save As dialog box. The title bar now contains your workbook's name.

Task 6: Closing a Workbook

Finishing with a Workbook

When you finish working on a workbook, you can close it and continue to work in the application. You can close a workbook with or without saving changes. If you have been working in a workbook and you try to close it, Excel asks you whether you want to save the workbook before it closes.

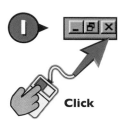

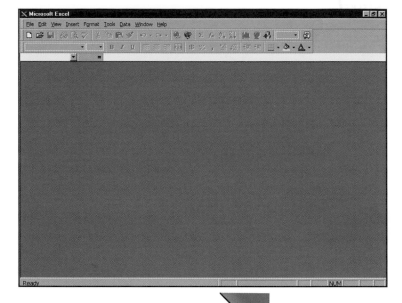

Click

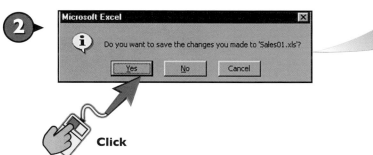

Click

✓ Buttons Available

When Excel has no workbooks open, only a few buttons are available on the Standard toolbar. Notice that as soon as you create a new workbook (see Task 7) or open a workbook (see Task 8), the buttons are available again.

 Click the **Close (X)** button on the title bar. If you have made any changes to the workbook, Excel asks you to save the workbook.

 Click the **Yes** button if you want to save changes; click the **No** button to close Excel without saving changes. Excel then closes the workbook.

Task 7: Creating a New Workbook

Start Here

1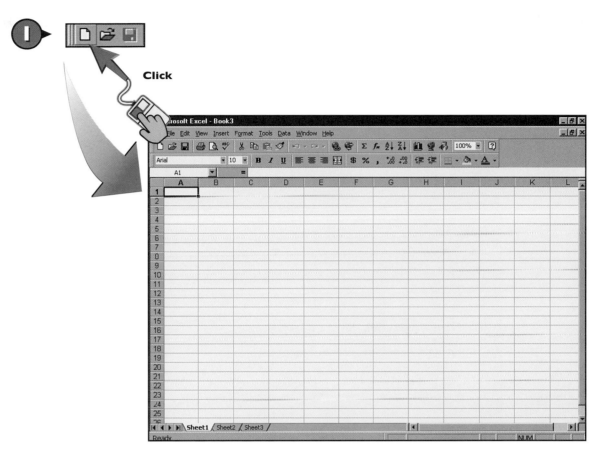

Click

Adding a Workbook

Excel presents a new blank workbook each time you start the program. You can create another new workbook at any time, however. For example, when you save and close one workbook, you might want to begin a new one.

 Default Filenames
Depending on how many new workbooks you have created while you are working in Excel, the default filename for each new workbook (Book1, Book2, Book3, and so on) automatically increases sequentially. If you exit and start Excel again, the numbers begin at 1 again.

1 Click the **New** button on the standard toolbar. Excel opens a new workbook with A1 as the active cell.

End Task

Retrieving a Workbook from Disk

Each time you want to work with an Excel workbook, you need to open it. You have many options to choose from in the Open dialog box. If necessary, click the **Look In** drop-down arrow and select a folder from the list. To move up a folder level, click the **Up One Level** button on the Open toolbar. If you double-click a subfolder, its contents appear in the Files and Folders list.

Task 8: Opening a Workbook

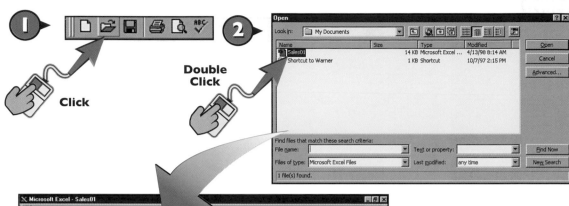

Start Here

Click

Double Click

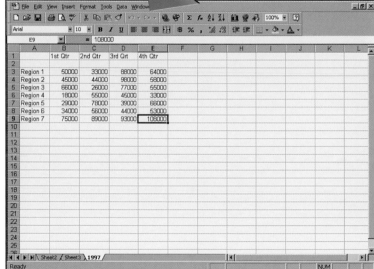

✓ **Look-In Option**
If you don't want to open your file in the **My Documents** directory, you can select the **Look in** drop-down list box and maneuver through your folders to open a file from a different location.

1 ▶ Click the **Open** button on the standard toolbar.

2 ▶ Double-click the file you want to open (for example, **Sales01**) in the Open dialog box. Excel opens the workbook.

End Task

Task 9: Switching Between Workbooks

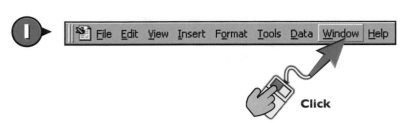

Click

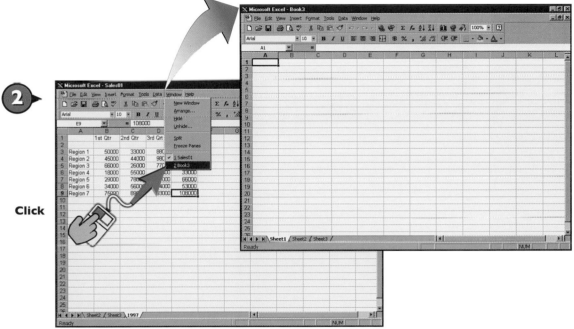

Click

Working in More Than One Workbook

When you become more familiar with working in workbooks, you might find it convenient to be working on more than one workbook at the same time. Excel makes it easy to switch from one workbook to another. To switch between workbooks, you need to have more than one workbook open. Task 8 told you how to open a workbook.

✔ **Switching Between Open Workbooks**
A quick way to switch between open workbooks in Excel is to simultaneously press the **Ctrl+Tab** keys.

1 ▶ Open the **Window** menu on the menu bar.

2 ▶ Click the workbook you would like to switch to. Notice that the workbook title is now displayed in the title bar.

✔ **Switching Between Worksheets**
To switch between worksheets, refer to Task 4.

Task 10: Viewing Multiple Workbooks

Seeing Several Workbooks on the Screen

Instead of constantly switching between workbooks, you can view multiple workbooks onscreen in Excel. This can be a very convenient feature if you are comparing two workbooks or working on two workbooks at the same time. You can have more than two workbooks open at a time, and you can also resize their windows. The workbook displaying a darker title bar is considered the active workbook. The active cell is visible in the active workbook.

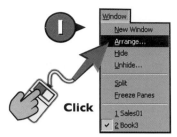

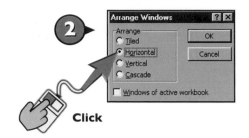

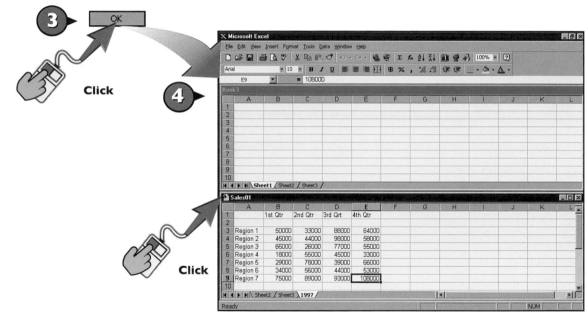

✓ Maximizing One Workbook

To return to viewing only one workbook (maximizing the workbook), double-click on the title bar of the workbook in which you want to work.

1 Choose **Window, Arrange**.

2 In the Arrange Windows dialog box choose how you want the windows arranged (for example, **Horizontal**).

3 Choose **OK**.

4 Click on the title bar or in the body of the workbook you want to work in to make it the active worksheet.

Task 11: Inserting Rows

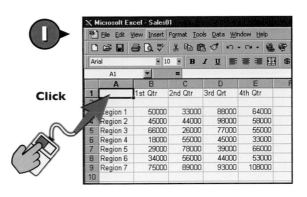

Click

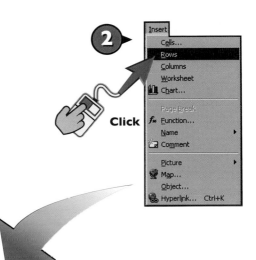

Click

Adding Rows

You can insert extra rows to make more room for additional data or formulas. Adding more rows, which gives the appearance of adding space between rows, can also make the worksheet easier to read.

① Click the cell you want to add a row above (for example, **A1**).

② Choose **Insert, Rows** to insert a row above the column titles.

 Automatic Formula Row Updates
When you insert a new row, Excel automatically updates any formulas affected by the insertion (see Part 6, "Working with Formulas and Functions," for more information).

Task 12: Inserting Columns

Adding Columns

You can insert extra columns to make room for more data or formulas. Adding more space between columns also makes the worksheet easier to read.

Start Here

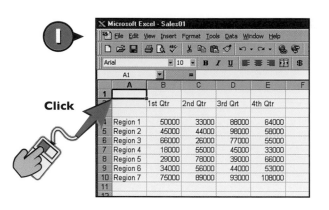

Click

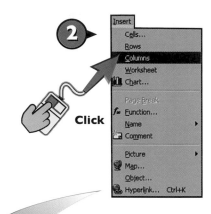

Click

Automatic Formula Column Updates

When you insert a new column, Excel automatically updates any formulas affected by the insertion (see Part 6 for more information).

I Click the cell you want to add a column to the left of (for example, **A1**).

2 Choose **Insert, Columns** to insert a column to the left of the row titles.

End Task

Task 13: Inserting Cells

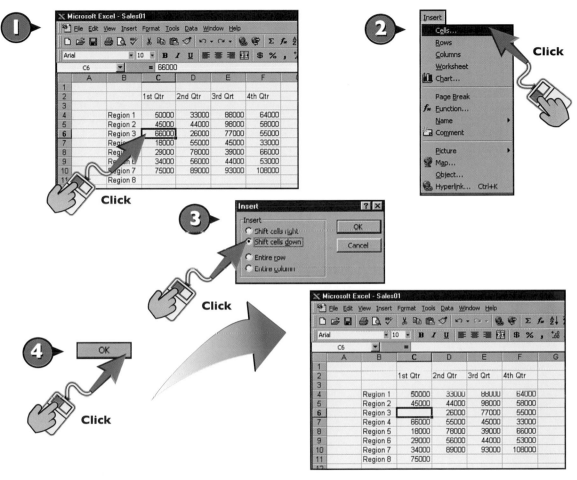

Adding Cells

Perhaps while you were entering data into your worksheet, you noticed that you typed the wrong amount of information. For example, suppose you have eight sales regions. You only keyed in seven regions, and keyed in the wrong first-quarter data for Region 3. To avoid retyping all the data again, you can insert cells and shift the current cells to their correct locations.

1 Click the cell where you want to insert a cell (for example, **C3**).

2 Choose **Insert, Cells**.

3 In the Insert dialog box choose how you want the current cells placed (for example, **Shift cells down**).

4 Choose **OK** and type the rest of the missing data.

✔ **Using the Shortcut Menu**
Another way to insert a cell is to right-click on a cell and choose **Insert** from the shortcut menu to open the Insert dialog box.

Choosing Cells to Work With

You will find it a common necessity to select cells—it's the first step in doing anything with them, such as copying and pasting, formatting, and even deleting.

Task 14: Selecting Cells

✓ **Using the Keyboard to Select Cells**

You can also select cells with the keyboard by pressing the **Shift** key and using the direction arrows to select the cells. In addition, you can press and hold the **Ctrl** key while you click on specific cells.

✓ **Select All Cells**

If you want to select the entire worksheet, click on the gray box above row 1 and to the left of column A.

Click the first cell in the range of cells you want to select (for example, **F11**).

Drag to the opposite corner of the range of cells you want to select (for example, **C4**).

Task 15: Copying and Pasting Data

Start Here

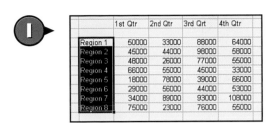

(1)

	1st Qtr	2nd Qtr	3rd Qrt	4th Qtr
Region 1	50000	33000	88000	64000
Region 2	45000	44000	98000	58000
Region 3	48000	26000	77000	55000
Region 4	66000	55000	45000	33000
Region 5	18000	78000	39000	66000
Region 6	29000	56000	44000	53000
Region 7	34000	89000	93000	108000
Region 8	75000	23000	76000	55000

(2)

Click

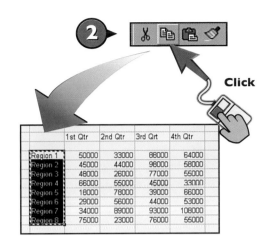

	1st Qtr	2nd Qtr	3rd Qrt	4th Qtr
Region 1	50000	33000	88000	64000
Region 2	45000	44000	98000	58000
Region 3	48000	26000	77000	55000
Region 4	66000	55000	45000	33000
Region 5	18000	78000	39000	66000
Region 6	29000	56000	44000	53000
Region 7	34000	89000	93000	108000
Region 8	75000	23000	76000	55000

(3)

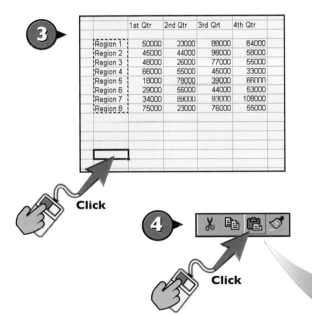

Click

(4)

Click

	1st Qtr	2nd Qtr	3rd Qrt	4th Qtr
Region 1	50000	33000	88000	64000
Region 2	45000	44000	98000	58000
Region 3	48000	26000	77000	55000
Region 4	66000	55000	45000	33000
Region 5	18000	78000	39000	66000
Region 6	29000	56000	44000	53000
Region 7	34000	89000	93000	108000
Region 8	75000	23000	76000	55000

Region 1
Region 2
Region 3
Region 4
Region 5
Region 6
Region 7
Region 8

Reusing Information

You can save the time and trouble of retyping information in the worksheet by copying cells and pasting them over and over again. You might, for example, want to copy a title or value from one cell to another cell, saving you time and keystrokes.

---

(1) ▶ Select the cells you want to copy (see Task 14 for instructions).

(2) ▶ Click the **Copy** button on the Standard toolbar. A dotted black line appears around the cells you are copying.

(3) ▶ Click the cell at the beginning of the location where you want to paste the cell data.

(4) ▶ Click the **Paste** button on the Standard toolbar. A copy of the cells appears in the new location.

End Task

✔ **Keyboard Copy and Paste Commands**
You also can use the simultaneous key combinations of **Ctrl+C** and **Ctrl+V** to select the Copy and Paste commands, respectively.

Task 16: Moving Data

Putting Data Somewhere Else

Excel will let you move information from one cell and place it into another cell. You do not have to go to the new cell and enter the same data and then erase the data in the old location. For example, you might want to move data in a worksheet because the layout of the worksheet has changed.

Start Here

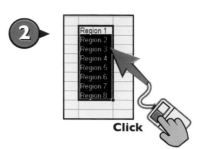
Click

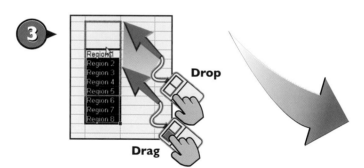
Drop

Drag

WARNING
If you move the wrong data or move the data to the wrong location, click the **Undo** button on the Standard toolbar to undo the most recent move. Then start over.

Select the cells you want to move (see Task 14 for instructions).

Click on the border of the selected cells. The pointer turns into an arrow.

Drag the cells to the beginning of the range where you want to paste the cell data and release the mouse button.

End Task

Task 17: Overwriting and Deleting Data

Start Here

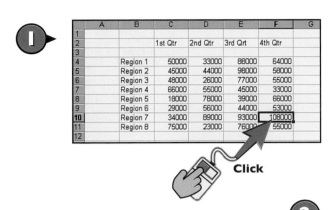

1

	A	B	C	D	E	F	G
1							
2			1st Qtr	2nd Qtr	3rd Qrt	4th Qtr	
3							
4		Region 1	50000	33000	88000	64000	
5		Region 2	45000	44000	98000	58000	
6		Region 3	48000	26000	77000	55000	
7		Region 4	66000	55000	45000	33000	
8		Region 5	18000	78000	39000	66000	
9		Region 6	29000	56000	44000	53000	
10		Region 7	34000	89000	93000	108000	
11		Region 8	75000	23000	76000	55000	
12							

Click

Getting Rid of Data

Overwriting a cell means replacing the cell's contents with new data. Overwriting is handy when you want to correct typing errors or when a cell contains the wrong data. You can also easily erase the contents of a cell by using the Delete key.

2

	A	B	C	D	E	F
1						
2			1st Qtr	2nd Qtr	3rd Qrt	4th Qtr
3						
4		Region 1	50000	33000	88000	64000
5		Region 2	45000	44000	98000	58000
6		Region 3	48000	26000	77000	55000
7		Region 4	66000	55000	45000	33000
8		Region 5	18000	78000	39000	66000
9		Region 6	29000	56000	44000	53000
10		Region 7	34000	89000	93000	78000
11		Region 8	75000	23000	76000	55000
12						

3

	A	B	C	D	E	F
1						
2			1st Qtr	2nd Qtr	3rd Qrt	4th Qtr
3						
4		Region 1	50000	33000	88000	64000
5		Region 2	45000	44000	98000	58000
6		Region 3	48000	26000	77000	55000
7		Region 4	66000	55000	45000	33000
8		Region 5	18000	78000	39000	66000
9		Region 6	29000	56000	44000	53000
10		Region 7	34000	89000	93000	78000
11		Region 8	75000	23000	76000	
12						

WARNING

Be careful not to overwrite formulas if that is not what you intended. If you overwrite a formula with a constant value, Excel no longer updates the formula. If you accidentally overwrite a formula but you've saved your spreadsheet recently, you can reopen the spreadsheet to a version before you overwrote the formula. For more about formulas and formula errors, see Part 6.

1 ▶ Click on the cell you want to overwrite, making it the active cell (for example, **F10**).

2 ▶ Type the correct data into the cell (for example, **78000**) and press the **Enter** key.

3 ▶ Press the **Delete** key on the keyboard to delete data in a cell, such as the contents of cell **F11**.

End Task

Task 18: Undoing and Redoing Changes

Using Undo and Redo

Many times you will find you are making numerous changes to your worksheets and need to undo some of the changes. Excel enables you to undo changes and redo them so you can quickly see the differences between the two.

Start Here

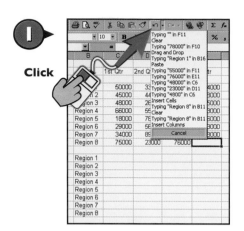

Click

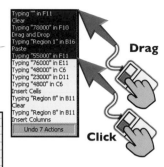

Drag

Click

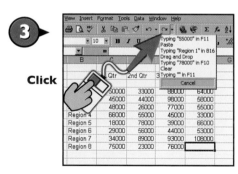

Click

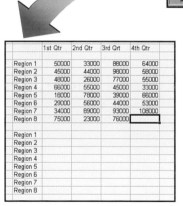

Drag

Click

✓ **Multiple Undo and Redo**

Instead of using the drop-down arrows, you can click the Undo and Redo buttons as many times as necessary to get your document back to the way you want it.

1 ▶ Click the **Undo** drop-down arrow on the Standard toolbar.

2 ▶ Drag over and click the specific items you want to undo.

3 ▶ Click the **Redo** drop-down arrow on the Standard toolbar.

4 ▶ Drag over and click the specific items you want to redo.

End Task

Task 19: Finding Data

Start Here

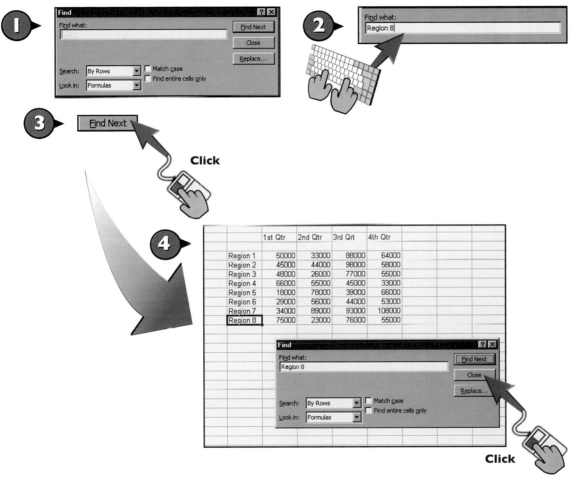

1

2

3 Find Next

Click

4

Using Find

You'll sometimes need to find specific information in a large spreadsheet. For example, suppose you want to quickly find the row that deals with sales data in Region 8. This worksheet is small, so it's not hard to find the information, but it serves as a simple example.

Click

1 ▶ Press the **Ctrl+F** keys to open the Find dialog box.

2 ▶ In the **Find what** text box type the data you would like to find (for example, **Region 8**).

3 ▶ Choose **Find Next**. Excel immediately finds the first instance of the information (if it exists in the worksheet) and makes it the active cell.

4 ▶ Choose **Close** to end the search.

✔️ **Using Find Next**
Another way to search for data is to choose **Edit, Find**. To continue searching for more occurrences of a Find criterion, click the **Find Next** button.

End Task

Page
97

Task 20: Replacing Data

Using Find and Replace

It might happen that you are working in a workbook and you notice you need to alter multiple cells of data. Perhaps you spelled a company name incorrectly throughout the workbook, or maybe you just want to enhance the data (for example, capitalizing a particular word throughout).

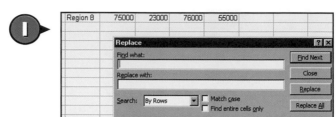

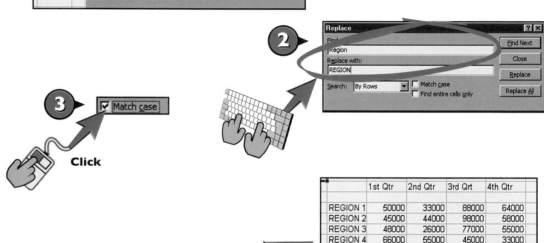

Click

Click

✓ **Search and Replace One at a Time**
You can search the document and replace each occurrence one at a time by choosing Replace instead of Replace All.

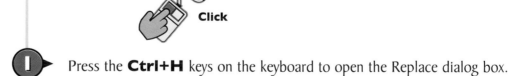

1. Press the **Ctrl+H** keys on the keyboard to open the Replace dialog box.

2. Type the data you would like to find in the **Find what** text box, and type the data you would like to replace it with in the **Replace with** text box.

3. Click the **Match case** check box so it contains a check mark.

4. Choose **Replace All**. Excel replaces all the occurrences.

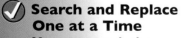

Task 21: Deleting Rows

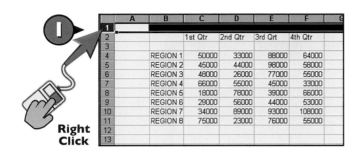

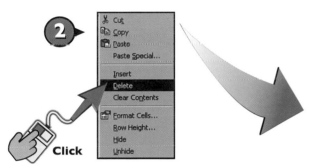

Removing Rows

You can delete rows from a worksheet to close up some empty space or remove unwanted information.

---

1 ▸ Right-click the heading of the row you want to delete (for example, **1**).

2 ▸ Click **Delete** from the shortcut menu.

 #REF! Error
If the #REF! error appears in a cell after you delete a row, it means you deleted a cell or cells that contained data your worksheet needs to calculate a formula. Undo the change; Task 18 told you how. For more on formulas, see Part 6.

Task 22: Deleting Columns

Removing Columns

You might want to delete columns from a worksheet to close up some empty space or remove unwanted information.

Start Here

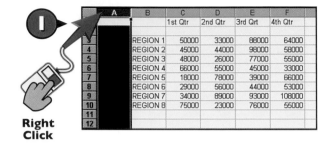

Right Click

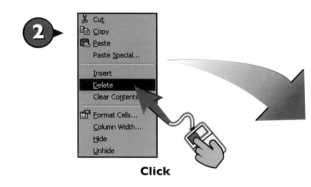

Click

✓ #REF! Error

If the #REF! error appears in a cell after you delete a column, it means you deleted a cell or cells that contained data your worksheet needs to calculate a formula. Undo the change; Task 18 told you how. For more on formulas, see Part 6.

I ▸ Right-click the column heading of the column you want to delete (for example, **A**).

2 ▸ Choose **Delete** from the shortcut menu.

End Task

Task 23: Deleting Cells

Start Here

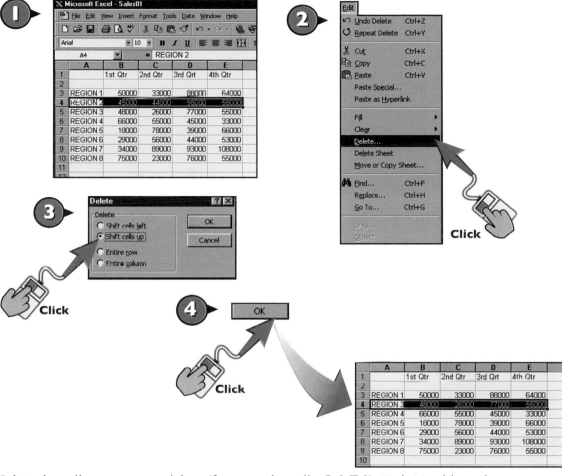

Click

Click

Click

Removing Cells

Sometimes when you're working with worksheets, you will find that data needs to be eliminated to keep the worksheet up to date. Perhaps your Region 2 is being closed out and the sales data is to be removed. Instead of leaving an extra row in your worksheet, you can delete the data in the specific cells and move the remaining data up into the next positions.

1. Select the cells you want to delete (for example, cells **A4:E4**). Task 14 told you how.

2. Choose **Edit, Delete**.

3. Choose how you want the current cells placed (for example, **Shift Cells Up** in the Delete dialog box).

4. Choose **OK**.

 #REF! Error
If the #REF! error appears in a cell after you delete, it means you deleted data your worksheet needs to calculate a formula. Undo the change; Task 18 told you how. For more on formulas, see Part 6.

End Task

Task 24: Tracking Changes

Keeping Track of Changes

Excel enables you to track changes that have been made to your worksheets. This is convenient when you are working on a team project in which multiple people are writing a report. For example, each person who adds data to the workbook can turn revision marks on so any changes they make show up in a different color from changes made by the other team members. The only time the colors won't be different is when two people use the same computer.

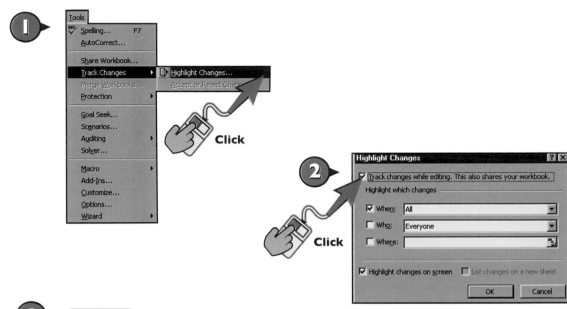

Click

Click

OK

Click

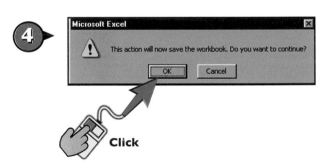

Click

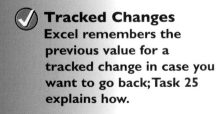
Tracked Changes
Excel remembers the previous value for a tracked change in case you want to go back; Task 25 explains how.

1 Choose **Tools, Track Changes, Highlight Changes**.

2 Click the check box next to **Track changes while editing**. **This also shares your workbook** in the Highlight Changes dialog box.

3 Choose **OK**. A message appears, telling you this action will save the document and asking if you want to continue.

4 Choose **OK**.

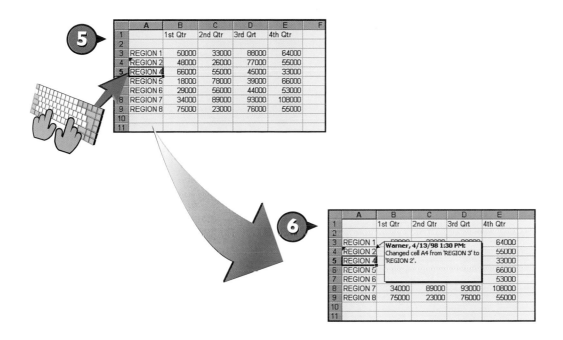

5 Type a change in a cell (for example, cell **A4**) and notice the cell now has a colored border. Press the **Enter** key when you finish editing a cell.

6 Place the mouse pointer over the revised cell and wait a second. A **ScreenTip** appears, showing the change that was made and who made the change.

End
Task

Keeping or Discarding Tracked Changes

When you are ready to finalize any tracked changes that have been made to a worksheet, you need to determine which changes you want to accept or reject. If you accept a change, Excel keeps it. If you reject a change, the previous text returns and the tracked change is deleted.

✓ No Note Markers

A note marker in the upper-right corner of a cell indicates there has been a change to the cell. Deselect the **Highlight changes on screen** check box in the Highlight Changes dialog box if you want to track changes to the document without using note markers. You can turn the note markers back on at any time by selecting the **Highlight changes on screen** check box.

Task 25: Accepting or Rejecting Tracked Changes

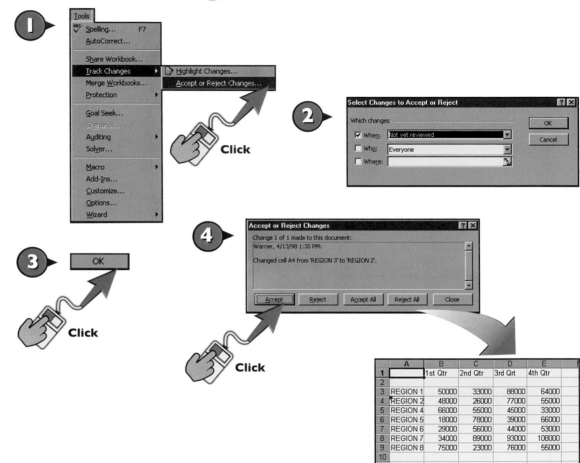

Choose **Tools, Track Changes, Accept or Reject Changes**.

In the Select Changes to Accept or Reject dialog box click the list boxes for **When**, **Who**, and **Where** you want to accept or reject a change.

Choose **OK**.

Choose **Accept** to keep the change, **Reject** to return to the original text, **Accept All** to accept all changes, or **Reject All** to reject all changes.

PART 6

Working with Formulas and Functions

In Excel, calculations are called formulas. Excel displays the result of a formula in a cell as a numeric value. Formulas calculate a value based on the values in other cells of the workbook.

Functions are abbreviated formulas that perform a specific operation on a group of values. Excel provides more than 250 functions that can help you with tasks ranging from determining loan payments to calculating investment returns. For example, the SUM function is a shortcut for entering an addition formula. SUM is the name of the function that automatically adds entries in a range. First you type =SUM(in either lower- or uppercase letters. Then you select the range. Finally, you end the function with an end parenthesis. Typing) tells Excel you are finished selecting the range.

Excel uses three types of cell references—relative, absolute, and mixed. The type of cell reference you use in a formula determines how the formula is affected when you copy the formula into a different cell. The formulas you create in this section contain **relative cell references**. When you copy a formula from one cell to another, the relative cell references in the formula change to reflect the new location of the formula.

An **absolute cell reference** is an entry in a formula that does not change when the formula is copied to a new cell. In certain formulas, you might want an entry to always refer to one specific cell value. For example, you might want to calculate the interest on several principal amounts. The interest percentage remains unchanged, or absolute, so you designate the entry in the formula that refers to the interest percentage as an absolute cell reference. The principal amounts do change, so they have relative cell reference entries in the formula. When you copy this absolute formula, the interest cell reference always refers to the one cell that contains the interest percentage.

A **mixed cell reference** is a single cell entry in a formula that contains both a relative and an absolute cell reference. A mixed cell reference is helpful when you need a formula that always refers to the values in a specific column but the values in the rows must change, and vice versa.

Tasks

Automatically Summing Cells

In a worksheet, if you want to show a sum of values from some cells, you could add them yourself and type the total. But if you then change any of the values, the sum becomes inaccurate. The beauty of Excel is that it can perform calculations for you by using formulas. Because a formula refers to the cells rather than to the values, Excel updates the sum whenever you change the values in the cells.

✅ Selecting Specific AutoSum Cells

If you don't want to AutoSum on the cells Excel selects for you, you can click on the first cell you want, hold down the Shift key, and click on each additional cell you would like to include in the calculation. When you finish selecting the cells you want to calculate, press **Enter** to see the result.

Task 1: Using AutoSum

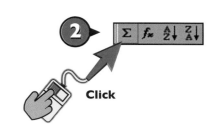

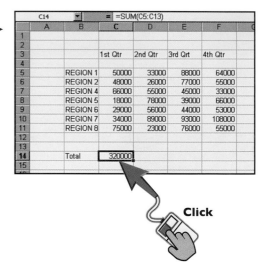

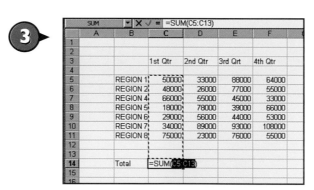

Click

1 Click cell **C14**. The result of the formula will appear in this cell.

2 Click the **AutoSum** button on the Standard toolbar.

3 Excel selects the most obvious range of numbers to calculate and indicates this with a dotted line around the cells. The Function Box displays the type of function (SUM). Press **Enter**.

4 Click cell **C14** to make it the active cell. Notice that the formula is displayed in the Formula bar.

End Task

Task 2: Entering a Formula

Start Here

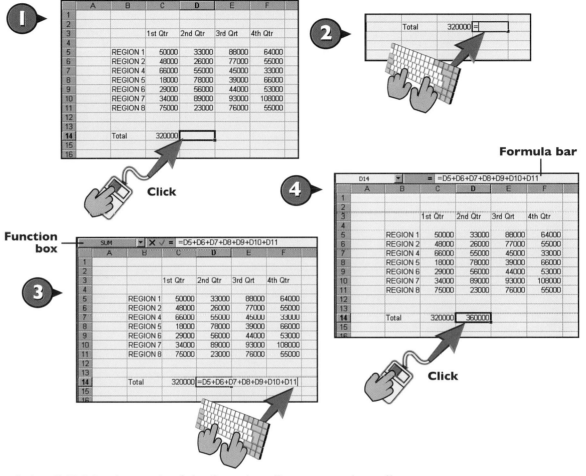

Function box

Formula bar

Typing Formulas

Sometimes you don't want to use AutoSum because you have specific cell references on which you want to perform calculations. In this instance, you can simply type the desired formula directly into the cell.

✓ **Altering Values**
After you enter a formula, you can change the values in the referenced cells, and Excel automatically recalculates the value of the formula based on the cell changes. You can include any cells in your formula; they do not have to be next to each other. Also, you can combine mathematical operations—for example, C3+C4-D5.

1 ▶ Click cell **D14**. The result of the formula will appear in this cell.

2 ▶ Type = (the equal sign).

3 ▶ Type **D5+D6+D7+D8+D9+D10+D11** and press **Enter**. Notice that the function box displays the type of function (SUM) and the results appear in the cell.

✓ **Canceling a Formula**
If you start to enter a formula and then decide you don't want to use it, you can skip entering the formula by pressing the Esc key.

4 ▶ Click cell **D14** to make it the active cell. Notice that the formula is displayed in the Formula bar.

End Task

Task 3: Entering a Function

Working with Functions

A function is one of Excel's many built-in formulas for performing a specialized calculation on the data in your worksheet. For example, instead of totaling your sales data, maybe you want to know the average of each quarter per region (Average function). Or, maybe you want to know in which quarter you had the largest sales (Max function) and smallest sales (Min function).

Start Here

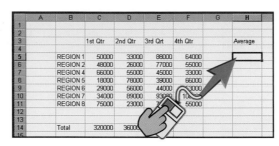
Click

Click

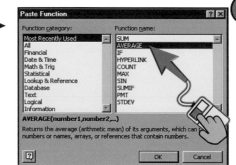

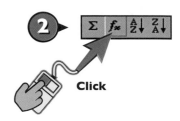
Click

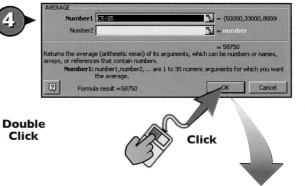
Double Click

Click

✓ Paste Function Dialog Box

The Paste Function dialog box offers many functions. Practice using different functions and see the results you get from your calculations. If the range is incorrect, type the range in the **Number 1** text box.

1 ▸ Click cell **H5**. The result of the function will appear in this cell.

2 ▸ Click the **Paste Function** button on the Standard toolbar.

3 ▸ Double-click the **AVERAGE** option in the **Function name** list box of the Paste Function dialog box. Excel selects a range of cells it determines you want to average.

4 ▸ Choose **OK**. The result appears in the active cell and the function is displayed in the Formula bar.

End Task

Task 4: Copying a Formula

Start Here

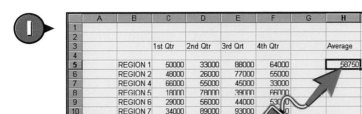

Click

Click

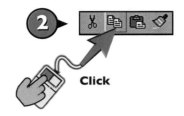

Click

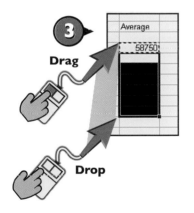

Drag

Drop

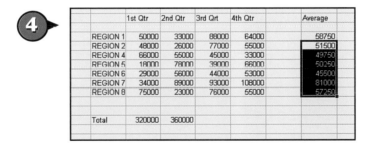

Reusing a Formula

When you build your worksheet, you often use the same data and formulas in more than one cell. With Excel's Copy command, you can create the initial data or formula once and then place copies of this information in the appropriate cells. You do not have to go to each cell and enter the same formula. For example, suppose you would like to find the average sales per quarter in other sales regions. Create the formula for the first region and copy it to cells for the other regions.

 Order of Operation
Excel first performs any calculations within parentheses: (1+2)=3. Then it performs multiplication or division calculations from left to right: (12+24)/(3*4)=3. Finally, it performs any addition or subtraction from left to right: (12+24)/(3*4)-2=1.

---

1 ▸ Click the cell that contains the formula you want to copy (here, **H5**).

2 ▸ Click the **Copy** button on the Standard toolbar.

3 ▸ Click and drag the mouse pointer over the cells where you want to paste the function. A dotted line surrounds the cell you are copying.

4 ▸ Press the **Enter** key to paste the function in the specified cells.

End Task

Task 5: Using AutoCalculate

Automatically Calculating Results

Perhaps you want to see a function performed on some of your data, but you don't want to add the function directly into the worksheet. For example, you want to find out what the lowest 4th-quarter sales were for all the regions in 1997. Excel's AutoCalculate feature can help.

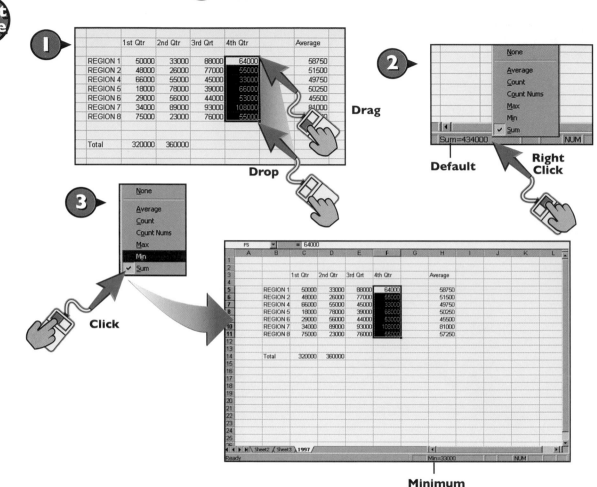

Start Here

Drag

Drop

Default

Right Click

Click

Minimum

✓ **Turning AutoCalculate Off**
You can turn the AutoCalculate feature off by selecting **None** from the AutoCalculate shortcut menu.

1 ▶ Click and drag the mouse pointer over the cells in which you want to AutoCalculate.

2 ▶ Right-click the status bar. Notice that the default AutoCalculate feature is to sum the numbers.

3 ▶ Select **Min** from the shortcut menu (to choose the minimum number in the selection).

End Task

Task 6: Fixing the #### Error

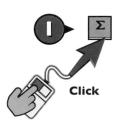

Click

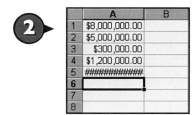

Understanding #### in a Cell

When a cell contains ####, the column is not wide enough to display the data. Widen the column to see the cell's contents.

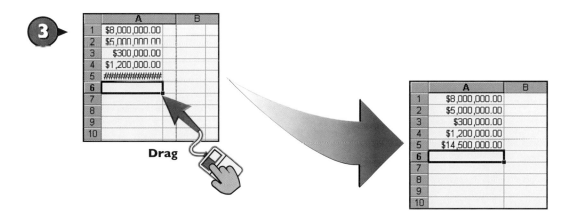

Drag

① Click the **AutoSum** button on the Standard toolbar.

② Press **Enter** and notice the #### error.

③ Click on the column border and drag it to increase the size of the column width. The error disappears.

✓ **Begin with Larger Columns**
It is a good idea to start out with columns larger than you need. Then you can decrease their size while you are formatting the worksheet.

Task 7: Fixing the #DIV/0! Error

Dividing by Zero

When a cell contains #DIV/0!, the formula is trying to divide a number by 0.

Start Here

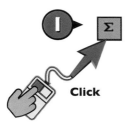
Click

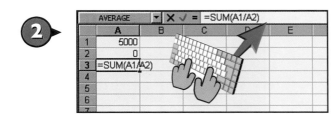

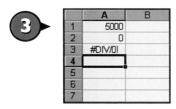

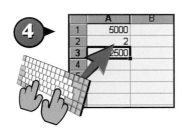

Delete Key
You can also press the **Delete** key in cell **A3** to remove the formula (refer to Part 5, Task 17 for instructions on getting rid of data).

1 ▶ Click the **AutoSum** button on the Standard toolbar.

2 ▶ Press **F2** and retype the formula as =SUM(A1/A2), which divides the value of AI by the value of A2.

3 ▶ Press **Enter**.

4 ▶ Type a different number in cell **A2** (for example, **2**). The error disappears.

End Task

Task 8: Fixing the #NAME? Error

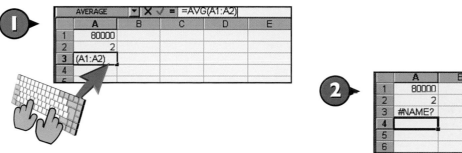

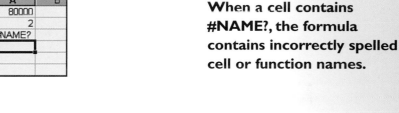

Recognizing Bad Cell References and Function Names

When a cell contains **#NAME?**, the formula contains incorrectly spelled cell or function names.

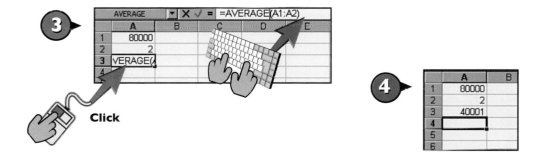

Click

Type the formula you want to use in your calculation (for example, **=AVG(A1:A2)**). (AVG is not the correct spelling for this function.)

Press **Enter**.

Click on cell **A3**, press **F2** on the keyboard to edit the cell, and retype the formula as **=AVERAGE(A1/A2)**.

Press **Enter**. The error disappears.

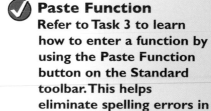

Paste Function
Refer to Task 3 to learn how to enter a function by using the Paste Function button on the Standard toolbar. This helps eliminate spelling errors in functions.

Task 9: Fixing the #VALUE? Error

Recognizing a Value Problem

When a cell contains **#VALUE?**, the formula contains nonnumeric data or cell or function names that cannot be used in the calculation.

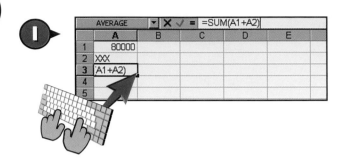

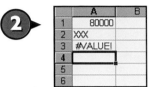

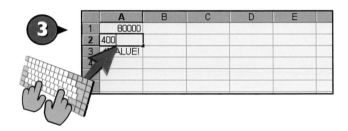

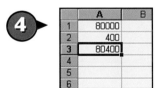

✓ **Overwriting Cells**
Refer to Part 5, Task 17 to make sure you are overwriting data in cells correctly.

① Type the formula you want to use in your calculation (for example, =**SUM(A1+A2)**).

② Press **Enter**.

③ Click on cell **A2** and type a number (for example, **400**) because cell A2 does not contain one.

④ Press **Enter**. The error disappears.

End Task

Task 10: Recognizing the #REF! Error

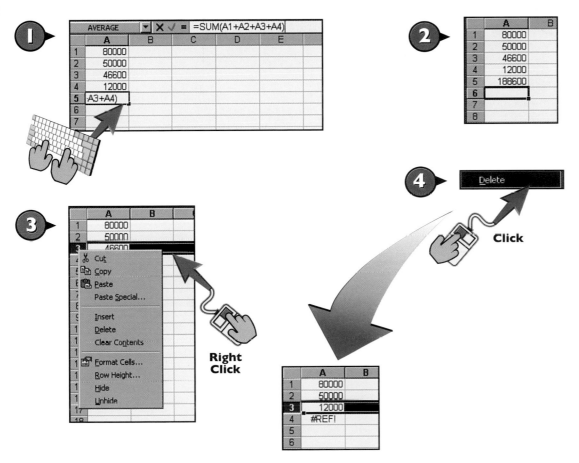

Understanding Bad Cell References

When a cell contains **#REF!**, the formula contains a reference to a cell that isn't valid. Frequently, this means you deleted a referenced cell. The best solution is to undo your action and review the cells involved in the formula.

① Type the formula you want to use in your calculation, such as **=SUM(A1+A2+A3+A4)**.

② Press **Enter**.

③ Right-click **Row Header 3**.

④ Choose **Delete** from the shortcut menu. Row 3 disappears.

✔ Undoing the #REF! Error

Remember, you can undo and redo your actions in Excel. This might help you find the action that made an illegal cell reference. Refer to Part 5, Task 18 for instructions on undoing and redoing changes.

Task 11: Recognizing Circular References

A Cell Can't Refer to Itself

A circular reference results when one of the cells you are referencing in your calculation is the cell in which you want the calculation to appear.

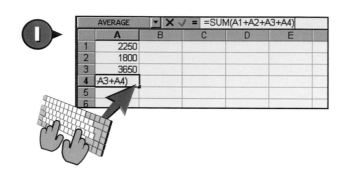

Start Here

✓ **Circular Reference Toolbar**
If you didn't intend to create a circular reference and you chose **OK** in the message box, the Circular Reference toolbar and Help will appear to assist you in correcting your actions.

Click

I ▶ Type the formula you want to use in your calculation (for example, **=SUM(A1+A2+A3+A4)**) and press **Enter**.

2 ▶ Choose one of the following in the Microsoft Excel message box: the **OK** button if you intend to create a circular reference, the **Cancel** button if you want to edit and correct your formula, or the **Help** button if you want Excel to help you create and understand circular references.

End Task

Working with Excel Worksheets

Formatting a worksheet means you can change the appearance of the data on it. With Excel's formatting tools, you can make your worksheet more attractive and readable. Numeric values are usually more than just numbers—they can represent a dollar value, a date, a percent, or some other value.

In Excel, you can print your worksheets by using a basic printing procedure, or you can enhance the printout with several print options. In this part, you learn how to print your worksheet from the Page Setup dialog box, but if you have already set up your print options and you're back to the worksheet, you can just click the **Print** button on the Standard toolbar.

Tasks

Task 1: Applying Styles to Numeric Data

Working with Styles

You can apply different styles to cells, depending on the type of data the cells contain. Using styles affects the way cells display data but does not limit the type of data you can enter. By placing data into a style, you can display it in a familiar format that makes it easier to read. For example, sales numbers tend to be styled in a currency format, and scientific data usually is styled with commas and decimal points.

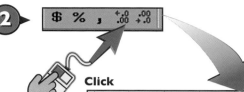

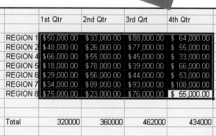

Click

Click

Click

✓ **Choose Other Styles**
Numerous other styles are available for applying to data. For a wider selection, select Format, Cells and click through the many Category options.

1 ▶ Select the cells you want. Part 5, Task 14 told you how.

2 ▶ Click twice on the **Increase Decimal** button on the Formatting toolbar.

3 ▶ Click the **Comma Style** button on the Formatting toolbar.

4 ▶ Click the **Currency Style** button on the Formatting toolbar.

End Task

Task 2: Applying Bold, Italic, and Underline

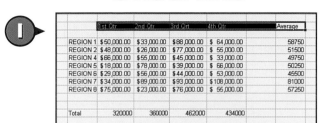

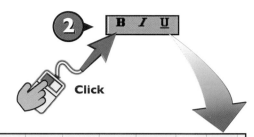

Formatting Data

You can format the data contained in one or more cells to draw attention to it or make it easier to find. Numbers attract attention when formatted with bold, italic, or underline. Indicating summary values, questionable data, or any other cells is easy with formatting.

Click

3 B *I* U

Click

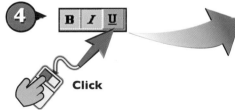

4 B *I* U

Click

1 Select the cells you want. Part 5, Task 14 told you how.

2 Click the **Bold** button on the Formatting toolbar.

3 Click the **Italic** button on the Formatting toolbar.

4 Click the **Underline** button on the Formatting toolbar.

✓ **Combination Formatting**
You can use several formatting techniques in combination, such as bold and italic or italic and underline.

End Task

Task 3: Changing Alignment

Aligning Data in a Cell

Excel provides several ways to format data. One way is to align data. The most common alignment changes you make will probably be to center, right-align, or left-align data. The default alignment for numbers is right-aligned; the default alignment for text is left-aligned.

Start Here

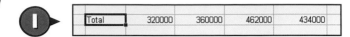

①

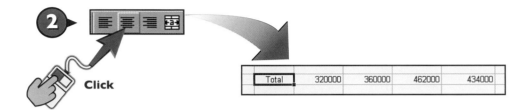

② **Click**

③ **Click**

④ **Click**

✓ **Default Alignment**
After you select text to align, if you click the same alignment button a second time, the cell returns to its default alignment.

① ▸ Select the cells you want. Part 5, Task 14 told you how.

② ▸ Click the **Center** button on the Formatting toolbar.

③ ▸ Click the **Align Right** button on the Formatting toolbar.

④ ▸ Click the **Align Left** button on the Formatting toolbar.

End Task

Task 4: Wrapping Text in a Cell

Start Here

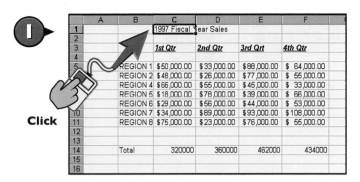

Click

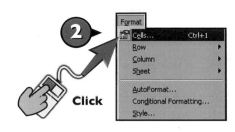

Click

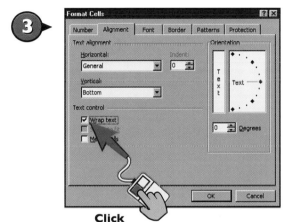

Click

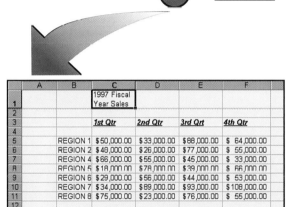

OK

Using the Wrap Text Feature

Excel provides several ways to format data. One way is to allow text to wrap in a cell. Many times a heading (row or column, for example) is longer than the width of the cell holding the data. If you are trying to make your worksheet organized and readable, wrap text so it is completely visible in a cell.

---

1 ▸ Select the cells you want. Part 5, Task 14 told you how.

2 ▸ Choose **Format, Cells**. The Format Cells dialog box opens.

3 ▸ Click the **Alignment** tab and select **Wrap Text** in the Text Control area of the Format Cells dialog box.

4 ▸ Choose **OK**.

Align Wrapped Text
You can align text that has been wrapped. Sometimes this gives a cleaner look to your text. Refer to Task 3 to learn how to align text in a cell.

End Task

Task 5: Using Merge and Center on a Cell

Merging Cells

Excel provides several ways to format data. One way is to use the Merge and Center feature. Columns of data usually have column headers, but they can also have group header information within a set of columns. For example, you might have four quarters' worth of sales data for the past two years, but want to have a header that distinguishes each set of quarters by their year.

Start Here

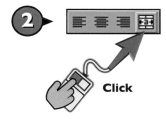

Click

✓ Undoing Merged and Centered Cells

You undo a set of merged and centered cells by first selecting the set of cells that are merged. Choose **Format, Cells.** Then click the **Alignment** tab and click the **Merge Cells** check box to deselect this option.

Select the cells you want. Part 5, Task 14 told you how.

Click the **Merge and Center** button on the Formatting toolbar.

End Task

Task 6: Changing Borders

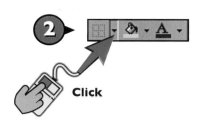

1997 Fiscal Year Sales

	1st Qtr	2nd Qtr	3rd Qrt	4th Qtr
REGION 1	$ 50,000.00	$ 33,000.00	$ 88,000.00	$ 64,000.00
REGION 2	$ 48,000.00	$ 26,000.00	$ 77,000.00	$ 55,000.00
REGION 4	$ 66,000.00	$ 55,000.00	$ 45,000.00	$ 33,000.00
REGION 5	$ 18,000.00	$ 78,000.00	$ 39,000.00	$ 66,000.00
REGION 6	$ 29,000.00	$ 56,000.00	$ 44,000.00	$ 53,000.00
REGION 7	$ 34,000.00	$ 89,000.00	$ 93,000.00	$ 108,000.00
REGION 8	$ 75,000.00	$ 23,000.00	$ 76,000.00	$ 55,000.00
Total	320000	360000	462000	434000

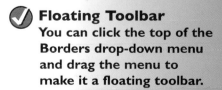

Click

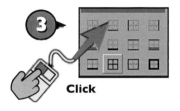

Click

1997 Fiscal Year Sales

	1st Qtr	2nd Qtr	3rd Qrt	4th Qtr
REGION 1	$ 50,000.00	$ 33,000.00	$ 88,000.00	$ 64,000.00
REGION 2	$ 48,000.00	$ 26,000.00	$ 77,000.00	$ 55,000.00
REGION 4	$ 66,000.00	$ 55,000.00	$ 45,000.00	$ 33,000.00
REGION 5	$ 18,000.00	$ 78,000.00	$ 39,000.00	$ 66,000.00
REGION 6	$ 29,000.00	$ 56,000.00	$ 44,000.00	$ 53,000.00
REGION 7	$ 34,000.00	$ 89,000.00	$ 93,000.00	$ 108,000.00
REGION 8	$ 75,000.00	$ 23,000.00	$ 76,000.00	$ 55,000.00
Total	320000	360000	462000	434000

Working with Cell Borders

Each side of a cell is considered a border. These borders provide a visual cue as to where a cell begins and ends. You can customize borders to indicate other beginnings and endings, such as grouping similar data or separating headings from data. For example, a double line is often used to separate a summary value from the data being totaled. Changing the bottom of the border for the last number before the total accomplishes this effect.

1 Select the cells you want. Part 5, Task 14 told you how.

2 Click the down arrow on the **Borders** drop-down menu.

3 Click the type of border you would like to apply (for example, **All Borders**).

✓ **Floating Toolbar**
You can click the top of the Borders drop-down menu and drag the menu to make it a floating toolbar.

End Task

Task 7: Changing Font Settings

Changing Typefaces

You can format data by changing the font used to display it. Changing the font gives data a different look and feel, which can help differentiate the type of data a cell contains. You can also change the font's size and color for added emphasis. For example, you can display subheadings as a different size font than main headings, or display different columns of data in different colors to differentiate them.

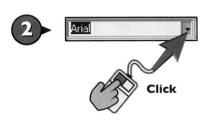

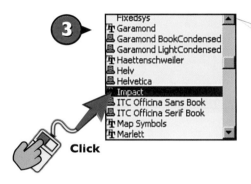

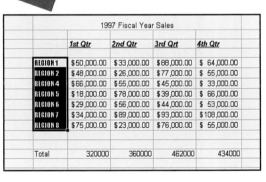

✓ Format a Portion of a Cell

To format only a portion of a cell's data, select only that portion and then change the font.

1 Select the cells you want. Part 5, Task 14 told you how.

2 Click the down arrow on the **Font** drop-down list box.

3 Click the font you would like to apply to the cells (for example, **Impact**).

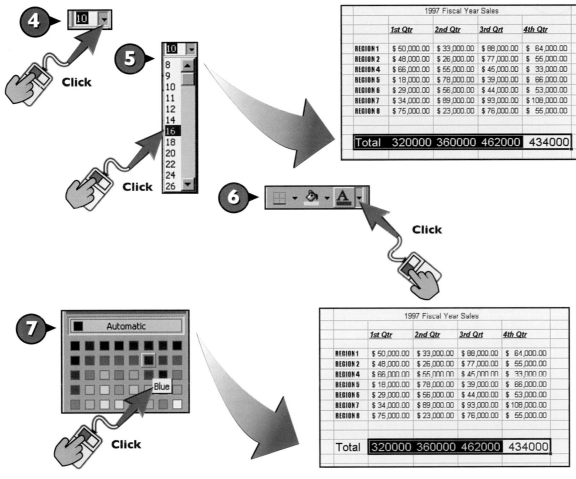

Click the down arrow on the **Font Size** drop-down list box.

Click the font size you would like to apply to the cells (for example, **16**).

Click the down arrow on the **Font Color** drop-down menu.

Click the font color you would like to apply to the cell (for example, **Blue**).

✅ **Preselecting Options**
You can also select a font color (or other options) before you begin typing. Then all the data in a cell will be that color.

✅ **Type in a Specific Font**
Instead of selecting a font size from the list box, you can click once on the Font Size list box and type the specific size you want.

Task 8: Filling Cell Color

Coloring Cells

Generally, cells present a white background for displaying data; however, you can apply other colors or shading to the background. In addition, you can combine these colors with various patterns for a more attractive effect. As with most formatting options, this can help emphasize more important data.

 Start Here

 1

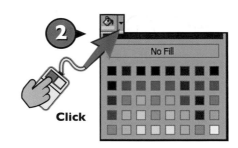 2 Click

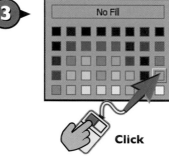 3 Click

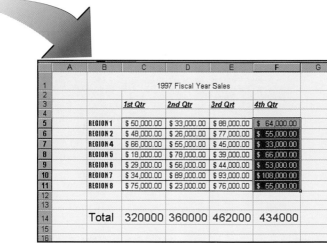

⚠ **WARNING**

Be sure a shading or color pattern doesn't interfere with the readability of data. The data still needs to be clear; you might need to make the text bold or choose a complementary text color.

1 ▶ Select the cells you want. Part 5, Task 14 told you how.

2 ▶ Click the down arrow on the **Fill Color** drop-down menu.

3 ▶ Click the shading or color you would like to apply.

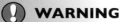
End Task

Task 9: Changing Cell Orientation

Start Here

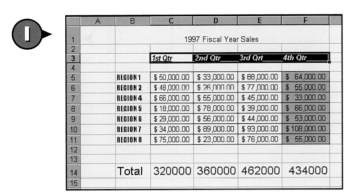

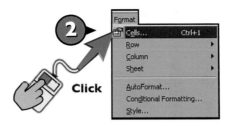

Click

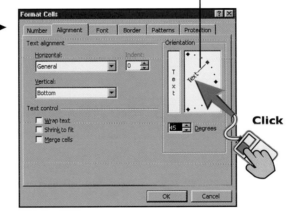

Orientation

Click

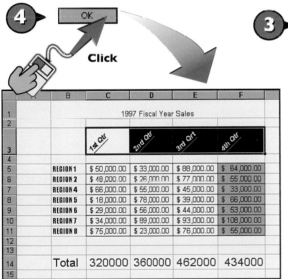

Click

Running Text at an Angle

Excel lets you alter the orientation of cells. The main reason for doing this is to help draw attention to important or special text. This feature can be convenient when you have a lot of columns in a worksheet and you don't want your column headers to take up much horizontal space.

1 Select the cells you want. Part 5, Task 14 told you how.

2 Choose **Format, Cells**. The Format Cells dialog box opens.

3 Click the **Alignment** tab and try the orientation options in the **Orientation** area.

4 Choose **OK**.

✓ **Rotating Data**
In the Orientation section of the Alignment dialog box, click on the half circle to change the angle at which data is rotated within the selected cell.

End Task

Task 10: Changing Row Height

Sizing Rows

Depending on the other formatting changes made to a cell, data might not display properly. Increasing the font size or forcing data to wrap around within a cell might prevent data from being entirely displayed or cause it to run over into other cells.

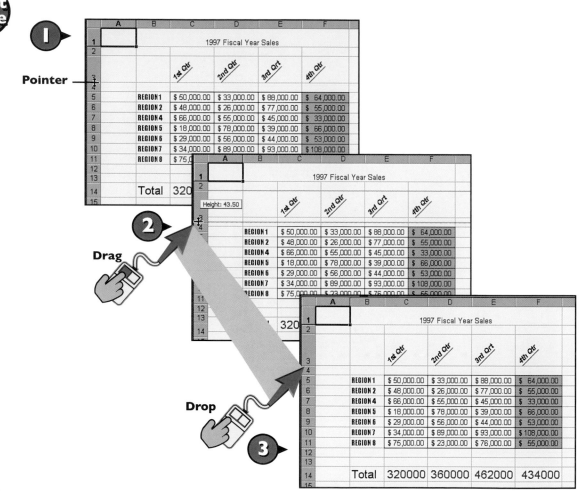

Start Here

Pointer

Drag

Drop

✓ Multiple Rows, Same Height

To make multiple rows the same height, click the mouse and drag over all the row headers you want resized. Then resize one of the rows. Each row becomes that size.

1 ▶ Move the mouse pointer over the bottom edge of the row header you want to alter (the pointer changes to a two-headed arrow).

2 ▶ Click and drag the row edge to the new size.

3 ▶ Release the mouse button to drop the line in the new location.

End Task

Task 11: Changing Column Width

Start Here

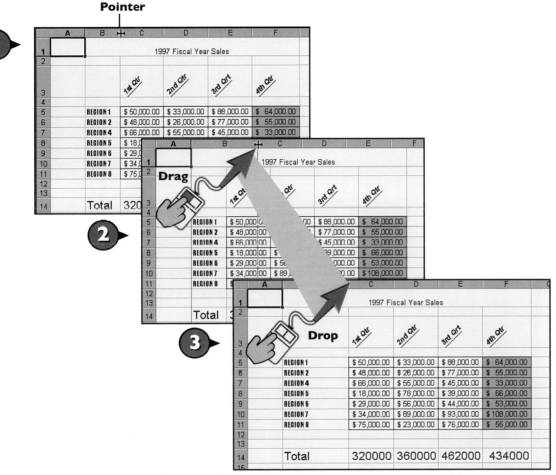

Pointer

1

2

3

Drag

Drop

Resizing Columns

Many times, data is too wide to be displayed within a cell. Excel provides several alternatives for remedying this problem. You can select columns and either specify a width or force **Excel** to automatically adjust the width of a cell to exactly fit its contents.

1 Move the mouse pointer over the side of the column header you want to alter (the pointer changes to a two-headed arrow).

2 Click and drag the column edge to the new size.

3 Release the mouse button to drop the line in the new location.

✓ **Multiple Columns, Same Width**
To make multiple columns the same width, click the mouse and drag over all the column headers you want resized. Then resize one of the columns. Each column becomes that size.

End Task

Task 12: Freezing Rows and Columns

Creating a Non-Scrolling Region

Many times your worksheet will be large enough that you cannot view all the data onscreen at the same time. In addition, if you have added row or column titles, and you scroll down or to the right, some of the titles will be too far to the top or left of the worksheet for you to see. For example, if you are reviewing data in column FF, it would be nice to see the row title of the cell you are referencing. To help, you can freeze the heading rows and columns so they're always visible.

 Click

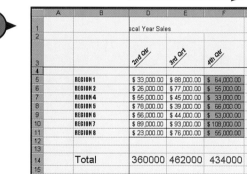

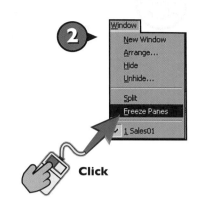 **Click**

✔ **Remove Frozen Panes**
To remove the freezing of columns and rows, choose **Window, Unfreeze Panes.**

1 Click in the cell to the right and below the area you want to freeze.

2 Choose **Window, Freeze Panes**.

3 Move through the worksheet (use the arrow keys) and notice that the rows and columns you selected are frozen so you can reference data with the appropriate titles.

End Task

Task 13: Using AutoFormat

Start Here

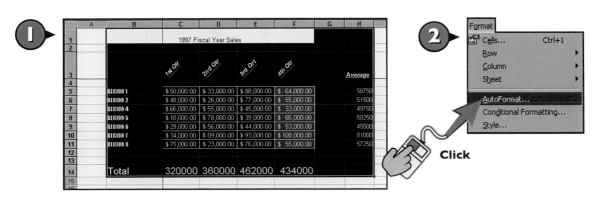

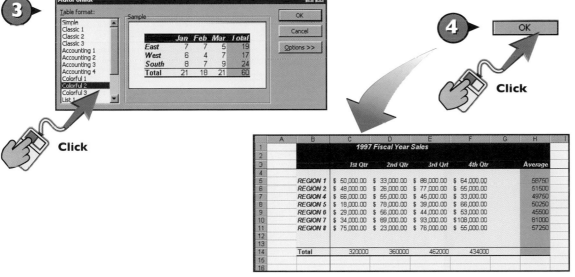

Automatically Formatting Worksheets

Using all the formatting capabilities discussed to this point, you could format your worksheets in a very effective and professional manner, but it might take a while to get good at it. In the meantime, Excel provides the AutoFormat feature, which can format selected cells by using predefined formats. This feature is a quick way to format large amounts of data and provides ideas on how to format.

1 Select the cells you want. Part 5, Task 14 told you how.

2 Choose **Format, AutoFormat**.

3 In the AutoFormat dialog box, click the table format you want (for example, **Colorful 2**). The Sample viewing area shows you a preview of the format.

4 Choose **OK** to apply the AutoFormat to your data.

✓ Modifying AutoFormat
If you find a format in the AutoFormat tool that doesn't quite meet your requirements, you can use that format but then make any necessary changes directly in the worksheet.

Task 14: Using Conditional Formatting

Formatting Cells Based on Content

At times, you might want the formatting of a cell to depend on the value it contains. For this, use Conditional Formatting, which lets you specify up to three conditions that, when met, cause the cell to be formatted in the manner defined for that condition. If none of the conditions are met, the cell keeps its original formatting. For example, you can set a conditional format such that if sales for a particular quarter exceed $100,000.00, the cell will have a red background.

When to Use Conditional Formatting

Use Conditional Formatting to draw attention to values that have different meanings depending on whether they are positive or negative, such as profit or loss values.

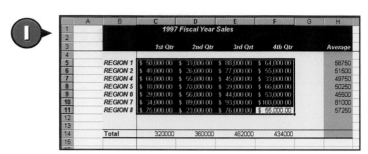

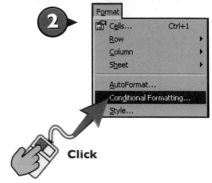

Click

Click

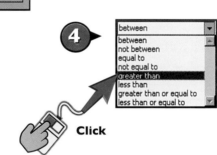

Click

1 Select the cells you want. Part 5, Task 14 told you how.

2 Choose **Format, Conditional Formatting**. The Conditional Formatting dialog box opens.

3 Click the drop-down arrow to select a cell value or formula condition (for example, **Cell Value Is**).

4 Click the drop-down list to select the type of condition (for example, **greater than**).

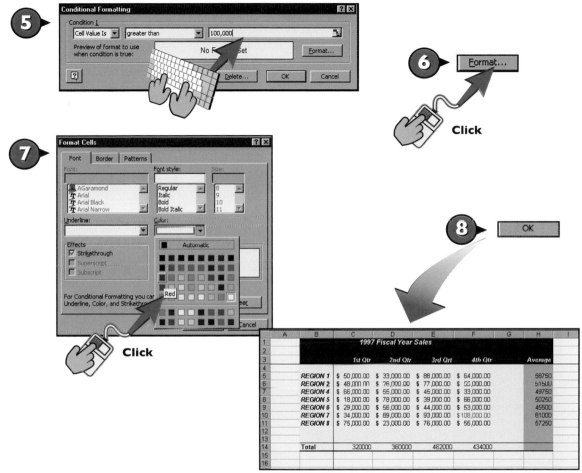

⑤ Type the value of the condition (for example, **100,000**).

⑥ Click the **Format** button for a preview of the format to use when the condition is met.

⑦ In the Format Cells dialog box, click the options you want to set (for example, the color **Red**).

⑧ Choose **OK** to accept your formatting changes and choose **OK** again to close the Conditional Formatting dialog box.

✅ **Format Painter Button**
You can copy the conditional formatting from one cell to another by using the Format Painter button. **Click the cell whose formatting you want to copy. Then click the Format Painter button. Finally, drag over the cells to which you want to copy the formatting.**

Graphing Your Data

Numeric data can sometimes be difficult to interpret. Using data to create charts helps visualize the data's significance. For example, you might not have noticed that the same month out of every year has low sales figures, but it becomes obvious when you make a chart from the data. The chart's visual nature also helps others review your data without poring over every single number.

Task 15: Inserting Charts

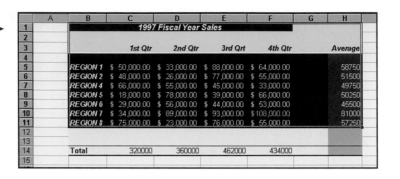

Click

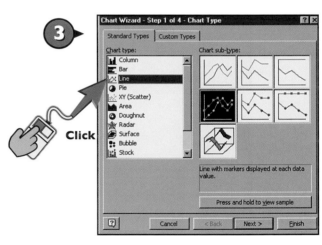
Click

Back and Cancel Buttons

At any time while using the Chart Wizard, you can click on the **Back** button to return to previous choices or the **Cancel** button to start over again.

1 ▶ Select the cells you want. Part 5, Task 14 told you how.

2 ▶ Click the **Chart Wizard** button on the Standard toolbar.

3 ▶ Choose the Chart type (for example, **Line**) and Chart subtype in the Chart Wizard dialog box. Then choose **Next**.

Next Step

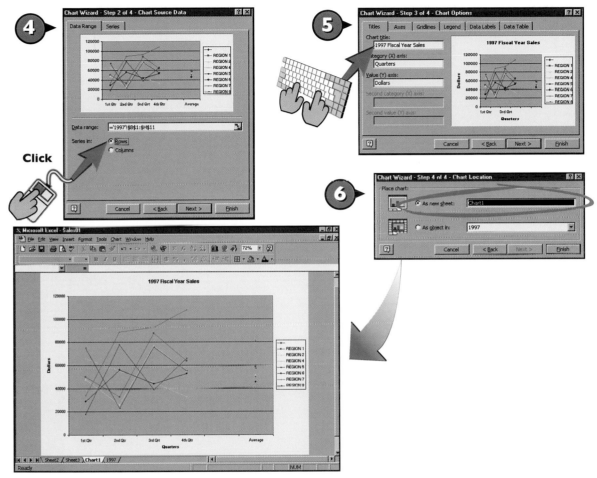

Click

4. Click Rows or Columns to choose which data to base the chart on. Here, click **Rows**. Then choose **Next**.

5. Type the various titles for the chart (for example, **1997 Fiscal Year Sales**). Then choose **Next**.

6. Choose the option for where you want to place the chart (for example, choose **As New Sheet**, titled Chart1). Then choose **Finish**.

 Chart Titles
Place your charts on a separate worksheet and give them meaningful titles. This way, a single worksheet can be used to visually summarize an entire workbook.

Task 16: Editing Charts

Changing Your Graphs

Charts are very useful for interpreting data; however, people look at data in different ways. To account for this, the appearance of charts in Excel can be quickly changed by using the Chart toolbar. The Chart toolbar makes it easy to change fonts, colors, and even the type of chart displayed.

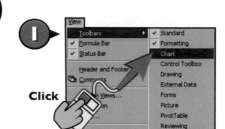

Click

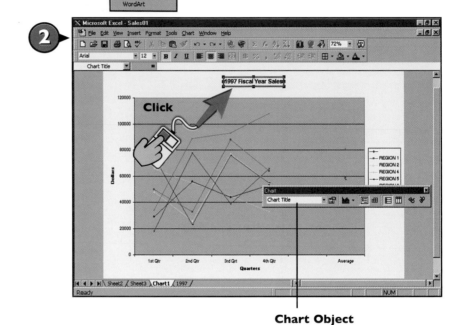

Click

Chart Object

✓ **Chart Toolbar**
If you have placed your chart into your data worksheet, you can simply double-click on the chart to initiate the Chart toolbar and begin editing the chart.

Choose **View, Toolbars, Chart.**

Click on any of the objects on the chart (for example, Chart Title). That object will now be displayed in the **Chart Objects** area of the **Chart** toolbar.

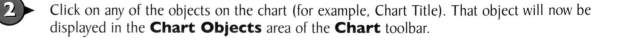

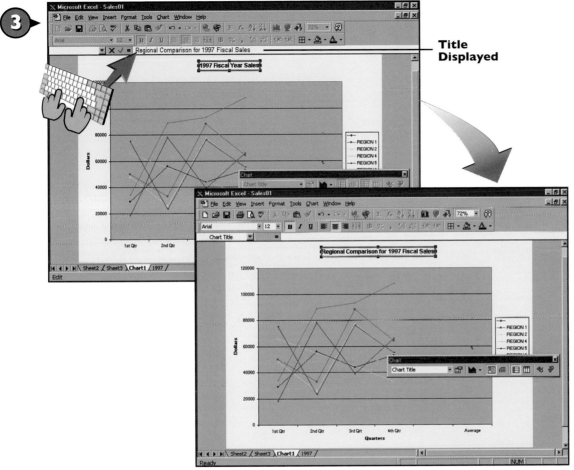

Title Displayed

3 Type the new Chart Title (for example, **Regional Comparison for 1997 Fiscal Sales**) and press the **Enter** key.

Task 17: Adding Cell Comments

Adding Notes to a Cell

Some cells contain data or formulas that require an explanation or special attention. Comments provide a way to attach this type of information to individual cells without cluttering the cells with extraneous information. A red triangle indicates that a cell contains a comment, which you can view in several ways.

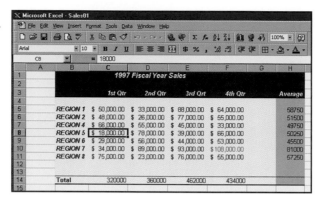

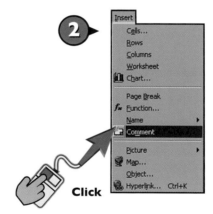

Click

 Select the cell you want. Part 5, Task 14 told you how.

 Choose **Insert, Comment**.

Next Step

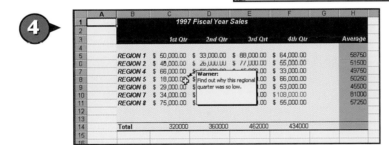

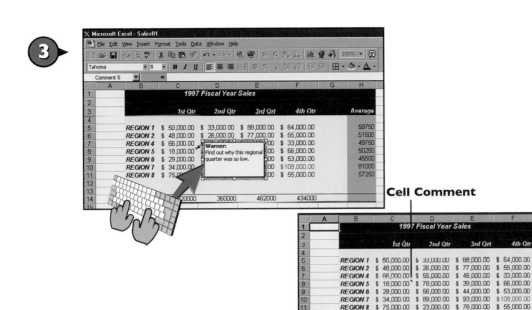

Cell Comment

3 Type the text into the comment area and click in the worksheet area to accept the comment. Notice that the cell's upper-right corner is now red to indicate the comment.

4 Move the mouse pointer over the comment marker in the cell to view the comment in a **ScreenTip**.

✔ **Working with Comments**
You can quickly edit or delete a comment by right-clicking the mouse on the cell that contains the comment marker and selecting either **Edit Comment** or **Delete Comment** from the shortcut menu.

Task 18: Inserting Clip Art

Adding Graphics to Worksheets

When you use Excel to generate reports or create presentation material, you might want to add some clip art graphics to improve the report's appearance or draw attention to a particular part of a worksheet. Office provides many pictures from which you can choose.

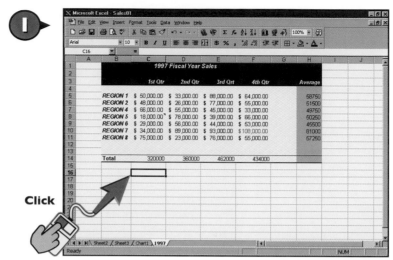

Click

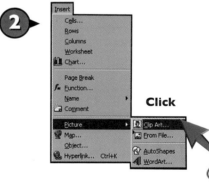

Click

✓ Microsoft Clip Gallery 3.0

It is easiest to view the pieces of clip art by looking at all the categories at the same time. If you are interested in selecting only clip art that is subject specific (for example, Animals), you can choose the specific category in the Microsoft Clip Gallery 3.0 dialog box and view only that type of clip art.

1 ▶ Click in a cell near where you would like to insert the clip art.

2 ▶ Choose **Insert, Picture, Clip Art**.

Next Step

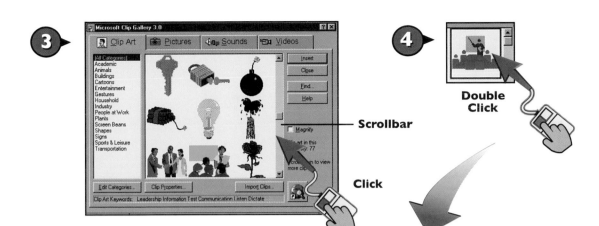

Scrollbar

Click

Double
Click

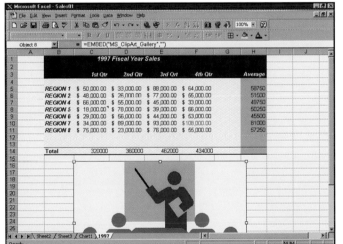

3 Click the **scrollbar** on the Microsoft Clip Gallery 3.0 dialog box to view the available clip art.

4 Double-click the clip art you want to insert.

End
Task

Task 19: Inserting Hyperlinks

Adding Jumps to Other Documents

When selected, *hyperlinks* move you to their specified document. That document can take many forms. For example, a hyperlink might open a Web page, a Word document, a sound or video file, a corporate database, or another Excel workbook. Because of this flexibility, hyperlinks can provide access to supporting material regardless of where it's located. A workbook on a network might have a hyperlink to documents in different cities or even different countries to help provide current information to anyone viewing the Excel data.

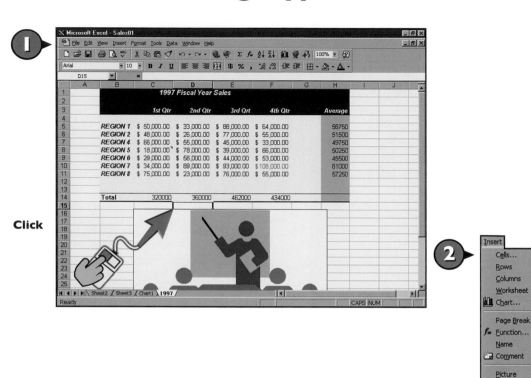

Click

Click

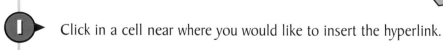

Click in a cell near where you would like to insert the hyperlink.

Choose **Insert, Hyperlink**.

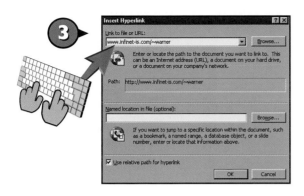

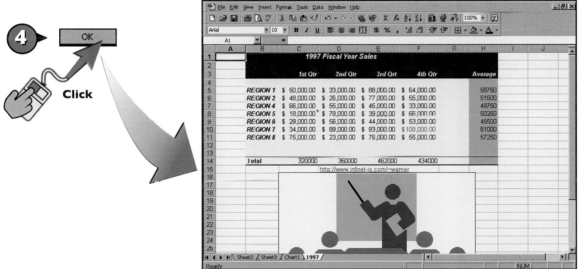

③ Type the path of the file or the URL of the Web page in the **Link to file or URL** text box.

④ Choose **OK** to enter the URL into the document.

✅ **Hyperlinks**
Hyperlinks can also contain email addresses, which begin with "mailto:." Clicking a hyperlink that contains an email address opens your default email client—ready to send a message to the address. Email hyperlinks make including contact information in workbooks very easy.

Task 20: Adding a Header and Footer

Start Here

Adding Information That Prints on Every Page

Headers and footers appear at the top and bottom of printed pages of Excel worksheets. Headers and footers can display the filename, date and time printed, worksheet name, page number, and more. Excel offers many standard headers and footers to choose from, or you can create custom headers and footers.

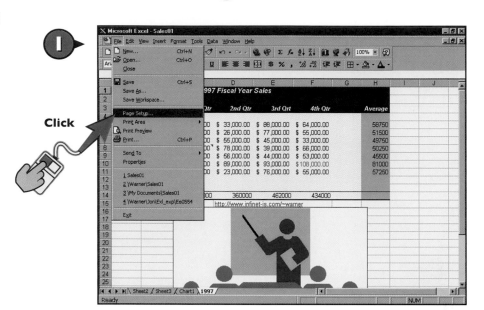

Click

Click

Choose **File, Page Setup**. The Page Setup dialog box opens.

Click the **Header/Footer** tab.

Next Step

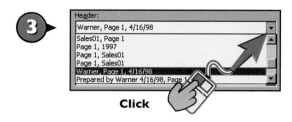

Click

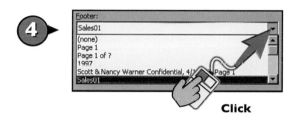

Click

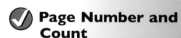

Click the **Header** drop-down list to choose from standard header options (for example, **Your Name**, **Page Number**, and **Date**).

Click the **Footer** drop-down list to choose from standard footer options (for example, **Filename**).

Choose **OK** to accept the changes. To view these changes, you need to be in Print Preview (see Task 23).

Page Number and Count

Add page numbers and the total page count to the header or footer to read, for example, "Page 2 of 7." Adding page numbers and count makes it easier to reorganize papers if they are dropped and alerts someone if some of the pages are missing.

End Task

Task 21: Changing Margins

Working with Margins

Margins affect where data is printed on a page. They also determine where headers and footers are printed. These might be changed to conform to company standards or to make room for a letterhead or logo on preprinted stationery.

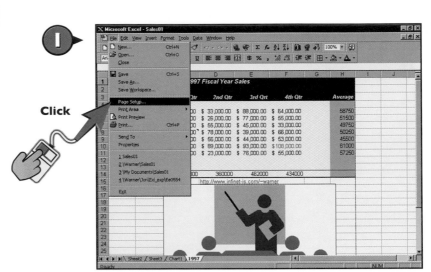

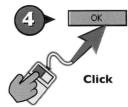

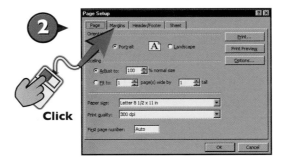

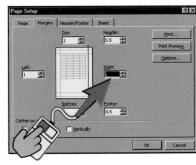

✓ Setting Margins

It is a good idea to set your margins before you begin working in a worksheet. Excel displays dotted lines along the row and column that borders the right and bottom sides of a worksheet's area within the page margins to let you know what data will print on each page.

1 Choose **File, Page Setup**.

2 Click on the **Margins** tab.

3 Click on the arrows in the **Top**, **Left**, **Right**, and **Bottom** boxes to set the margins (for example, set them all to **1** inch) and the **Header** and **Footer** boxes to set these margins.

4 Choose **OK** to accept the changes. To view these changes, you need to be in Print Preview (see Task 23).

End Task

Task 22: Setting the Print Area

Click

Choosing What to Print

Worksheets can cover a large number of rows and columns. Setting the print area enables you to specify exactly which rows and columns will print. The Print Area feature makes it possible to store the information for many reports on a single worksheet. When it is time to print one of the reports, you simply set the Print Area to include those cells that contain the report you want.

 Select the cells you want to print. Part 5, Task 14 told you how.

 Choose **File, Print Area, Set Print Area**.

✓ Print All on a Single Page

Setting the print area does not cause all information to be printed on a single page. To do that, use the **Scaling** option in the Page Setup dialog box.

 End Task

Task 23: Using Print Preview

Seeing What Your Printout Will Look Like

Workbooks with lots of data can generate large print jobs, possibly containing hundreds of pages. Waiting until all these pages are printed to verify that the information is printed correctly can cost a lot in both time and printing supplies. To help prevent printing mistakes, use Print Preview to ensure that all the necessary elements appear on the pages being printed.

Start Here

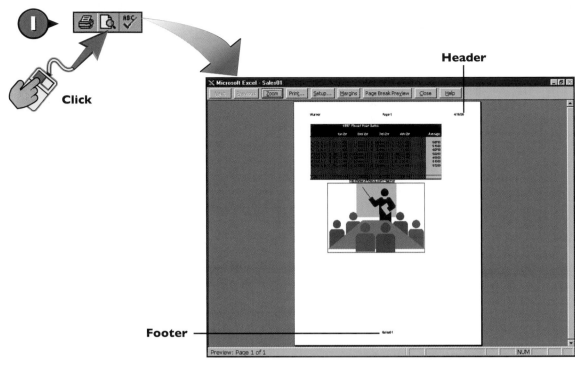

Header

Footer

Click

Click

✓ Margins

If you're using Print Preview and you decide you want to alter your margins, you can click the **Margins** button. The margin guides become visible. Select any of the margin or column guides to see how you can alter your worksheet.

1 ▶ Click the **Print Preview** button on the Standard toolbar.

2 ▶ Click the **Print** button to print the worksheet or the **Close** button to return to the worksheet.

End Task

Task 24: Printing Worksheets

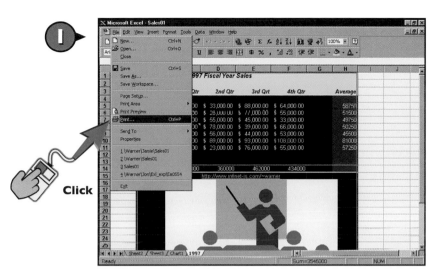

Click

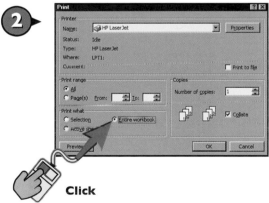

Click

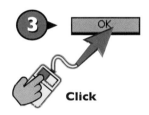

Click

Getting Hard Copy

Printing a workbook is quite simple, but setting the option for printing a workbook can be complex. The number of options that must be set before printing a workbook depends on the amount of data stored in the workbook, how it is arranged, and how much of it needs to be printed.

1 Choose **File, Print**.

2 Set printing options in the Print dialog box. For example, select **Entire workbook** in the **Print what** section.

3 Choose **OK** to print what you have selected.

✓ **Quick Print**
Clicking the **Print** button on the **Standard toolbar** prints your worksheet based on Excel's default options. Use Print Preview to see what is to be printed. Then make any necessary changes before printing the workbook.

End Task

PART 8

PowerPoint Basics

In PowerPoint, you create your presentation as just one file. That file contains everything you need—an outline of your presentation, your slides, audience handouts, and even your speaker's notes.

You can use PowerPoint to plan every aspect of a winning presentation. PowerPoint even helps you organize the ideas in your presentation through its AutoContent Wizard, which quickly creates your presentation, including a title slide and several slides containing bulleted lists.

Tasks

Task 1: Starting PowerPoint

Getting Started in PowerPoint

PowerPoint is designed to help business professionals create visually attractive presentations. You can also use it to create complex graphics for a variety of purposes. This flexibility—and especially the ease of use for non-artists—makes PowerPoint a great addition to anyone's software tools.

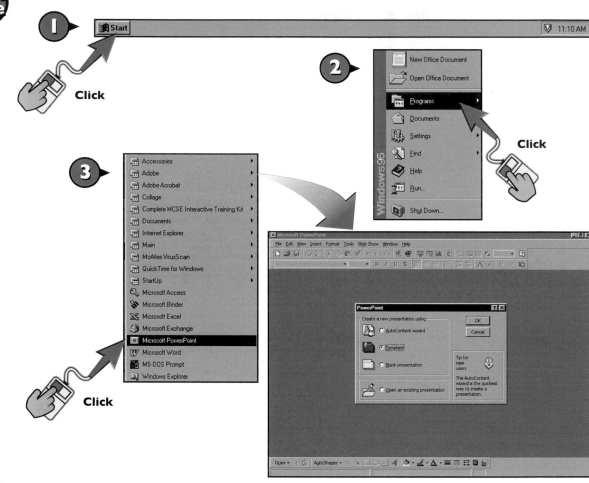

Start Here

Click

Click

Click

✓ Starting PowerPoint from a File

Another way to start the PowerPoint application is to double-click on a PowerPoint file in an Explorer window. The application automatically launches and opens to that particular file.

1 ▶ Click the **Start** button on the taskbar.

2 ▶ Move the mouse cursor to **Programs**.

3 ▶ Click on **Microsoft PowerPoint** to start the application.

End Task

Task 2: Starting a Blank Presentation

Start Here

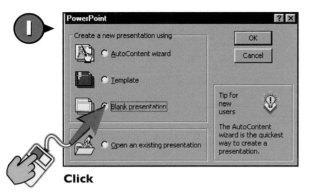

1 Click

2 Click

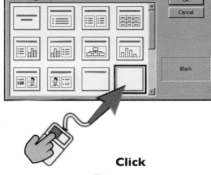

3 Click

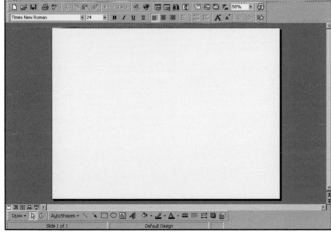

4 Click

Making a Presentation from Scratch

For the most control over your PowerPoint presentations, start with a blank presentation and add only the items you want. This gives you the opportunity to use your creativity. It also allows you to use PowerPoint for creating files beyond basic business presentations. Your imagination is the only limitation.

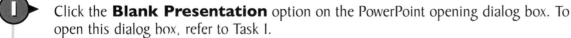

1 ▶ Click the **Blank Presentation** option on the PowerPoint opening dialog box. To open this dialog box, refer to Task 1.

2 ▶ Choose **OK**.

3 ▶ Click the **Blank** slide in the **Choose an AutoLayout** selection area.

4 ▶ Choose **OK**.

✔ **Applying Templates**
You can apply a template to your presentation at any time, even if you have already created your presentation. See Task 4 to learn how to build presentations.

End Task

Task 3: Starting an AutoContent Presentation

Start Here

Using the AutoContent Wizard

Sometimes it just seems impossible to get started on a presentation. You don't even know where to start. For these situations, use the AutoContent Wizard. It asks you a series of questions and uses your answers to start a presentation for you. You fill in the details.

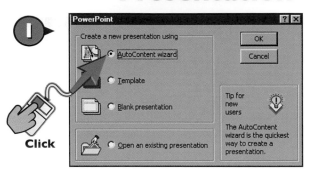

Click

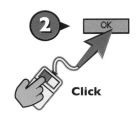

Click

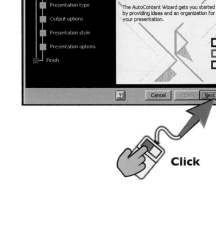

Click

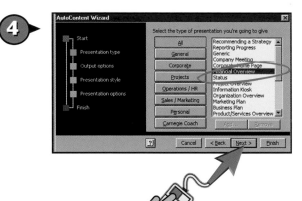

Click

✅ **Using the Back and Cancel Buttons**
You can click the **Back** button on the AutoContent Wizard dialog box at any time to alter previously entered information. Keep in mind that you must click the particular option you want to alter before you retype any changes. You can stop the AutoContent Wizard's progress at any time by clicking the **Cancel** button.

1 Click the **AutoContent wizard** option in the PowerPoint opening dialog box. To open this dialog box, refer to Task 1.

2 Choose **OK**.

3 Read the welcome information in the AutoContent Wizard dialog box and then choose **Next**.

4 Click the kind of presentation you want to create (for example, **Financial Overview**), and then choose **Next**.

Next Step

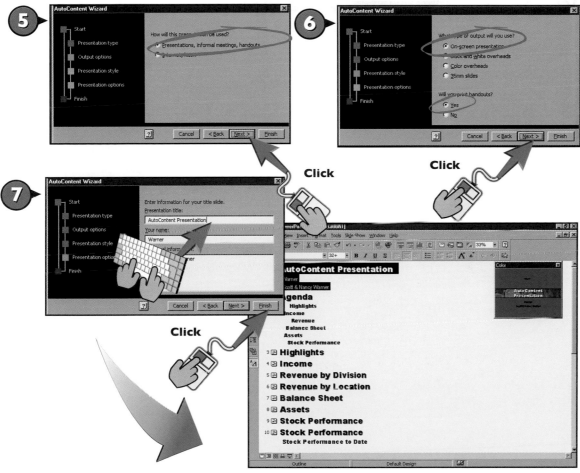

Click

Click

Click

5 Click the **Presentations, informal meetings, handouts** option and then choose **Next** from the Output options.

6 From the Presentation style options, choose **On-screen presentation** for the type of output and click **Yes** for printing handouts. Then choose **Next**.

7 Type the Presentation options—**Presentation title**, **Your name**, and any **Additional information**— and then click the **Finish** button.

✓ Create Complex Presentations
If you like the way the AutoContent Wizard gets a presentation off to a quick start, but you need more complex presentations, use the wizard to create the core of your presentation. Then add to your presentation by using templates or creating new slides from scratch.

End Task

Task 4: Starting a Template Presentation

Creating a Presentation from a Template

PowerPoint comes with several presentation templates that were created for various types of presentations and situations. These templates have basic artistic features and usually a skeleton outline you can fill in or expand on. Take advantage of these to quickly create presentations.

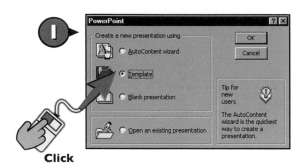

Click

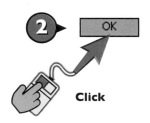

Click

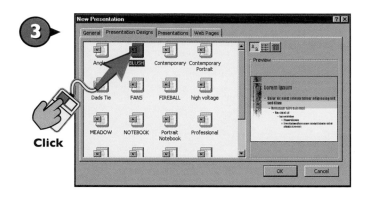

Click

Click

✓ **Choose an AutoLayout**
Numerous options are available in the Choose an AutoLayout selection area. Practice selecting different options and adding text and graphics to the presentations.

1 ▸ Click the **Template** option on the PowerPoint opening dialog box. To open this dialog box, refer to Tasks.

2 ▸ Click the **OK** button.

3 ▸ Select a template from the **Presentation Designs** tab of the New Presentation dialog box (for example, **Blush**).

4 ▸ Click the **OK** button.

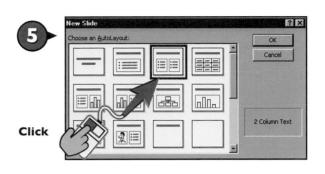

5

Click

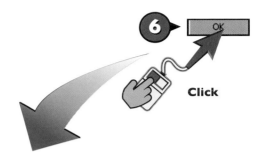

6

Click

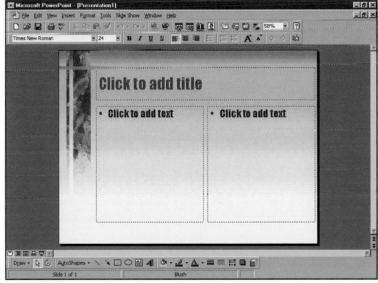

5 In the **Choose an AutoLayout** selection area, click the type of slide you would like to begin with (for example, **2 Column Text**).

6 Choose **OK**.

Creating a New Presentation
If you didn't just start PowerPoint, you have to create a new presentation and select a template from the Presentation Design tab of the New Presentation dialog box. See Task 9 for information on how to begin a new presentation while working in PowerPoint.

Task 5: Using Outline View

Working with Your Presentation's Outline

For some presentations, the art is secondary or possibly even nonexistent. Because presentations like this rely mainly on their text, the text should receive the most attention. Create text-based presentations by using the Outline view, which displays only the text for the presentation. Outline view enables you to quickly lay out main ideas in your presentation.

✅ **Show Formatting**
Clicking the **Show Formatting** button on the Outline toolbar shows text in the fonts and font sizes the wizard selected for you (or, if that's how the outline already looked, this button hides the formatting instead). The formatted text looks nice, but it's easier to create your presentation without the formatting, where you can see more text in the window.

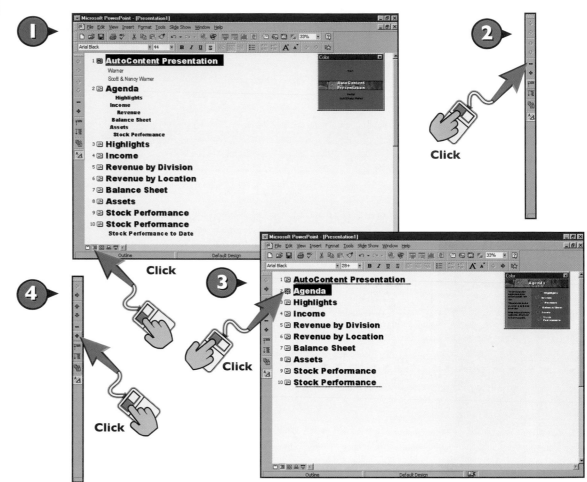

① Click the **Outline View** button in the lower-left corner of the presentation area.

② Click the **Collapse** button on the Outline toolbar.

③ Move the mouse pointer to one of the slides (here, the **Agenda** slide) and click when the pointer becomes a four-headed arrow.

④ Click the **Expand** button on the Outline toolbar.

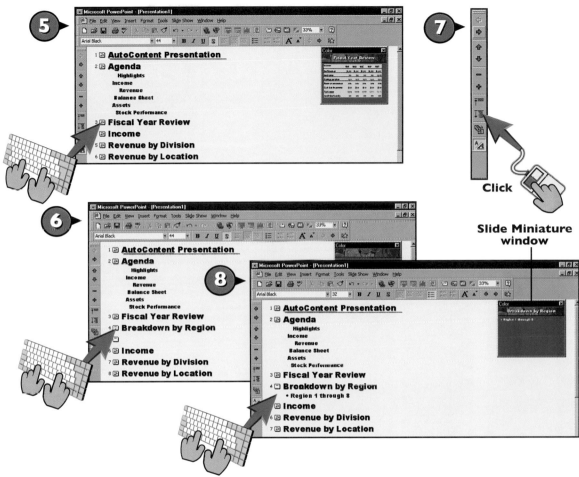

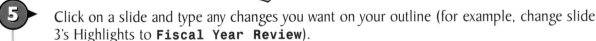

Click

Slide Miniature window

End Task

Page 163

5 Click on a slide and type any changes you want on your outline (for example, change slide 3's Highlights to `Fiscal Year Review`).

6 Press the **Enter** key at the end of slide 3's **Fiscal Year Review** and type a title for the new slide 4 (for example, `Breakdown by Region`). Press the **Enter** key again.

7 Click the **Demote** button on the Outline toolbar to change the new slide 5 to a main topic under slide 4.

8 Type the information you want on slide 4. PowerPoint automatically places the text in the Slide Miniature window.

✅ **Review Your Presentations**
Large presentations with lots of graphics present many opportunities for misspelled words or missing sections. Review presentations in Outline view when they are finished. Outline view enables you to review text without being concerned about the accompanying graphics.

Task 6: Working in Different Views

Using Views

PowerPoint provides several ways to view presentations while creating or modifying them. Switching between these views is simple, and you should do it frequently. Each view provides a different perspective on a presentation, which could lead to new ideas.

Start Here

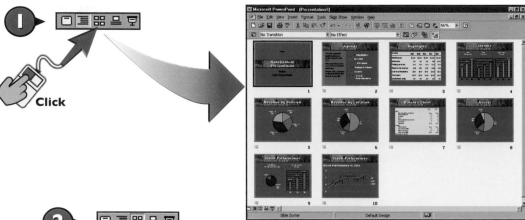

① Click

② Click

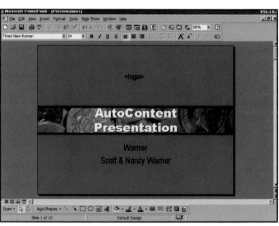

① Click the **Slide Sorter View** button. This enables you to rearrange your slides.

② Click the **Slide View** button. You can add both text and art on a slide-by-slide basis.

Next
Step

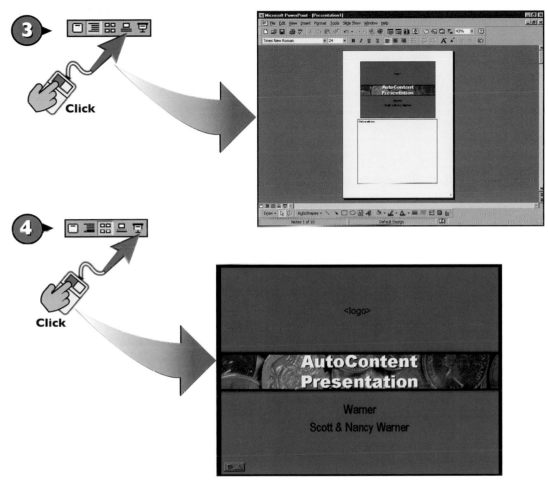

3 Click the **Notes Pages View** button. You can type speaker notes on each slide.

4 Click the **Slide Show** button. This enables you to view your slides as they would appear in a slide show. (Press the **Esc** key to return from the Slide Show view.)

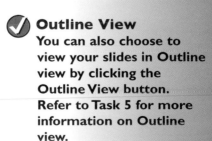

Outline View
You can also choose to view your slides in Outline view by clicking the Outline View button. Refer to Task 5 for more information on Outline view.

Storing a Presentation on Disk

PowerPoint provides more than one method for saving presentations. You should take advantage of at least one of these often. Unsaved presentations are lost if anything happens to your application or computer.

Task 7: Saving a Presentation

Start Here

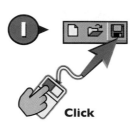
1 Click

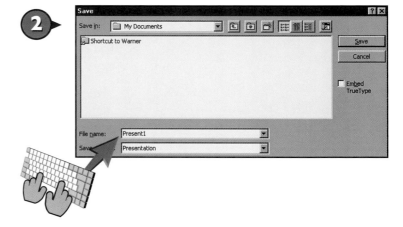
2

3 Save
Click

✓ **Save In Options**
If you don't want to save your file in the My Documents directory, click the arrow in the Save in drop-down list box and maneuver through your directories to save the file in a different location.

1 Click the **Save** button on the Standard toolbar. If you have never saved this presentation, the Save As dialog box appears with a default filename (Presentation).

2 Type a different filename if you want (for example, **Present1**).

3 Click the **Save** button.

End Task

Task 8: Closing a Presentation

Start Here

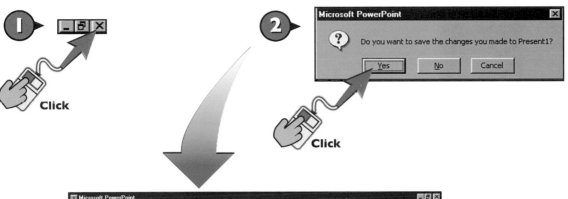

Click

Click

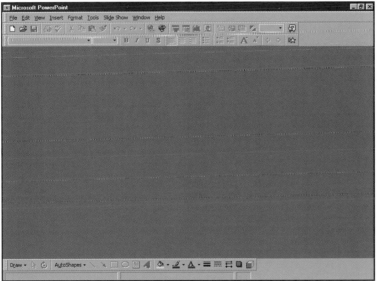

Finishing Work on a Presentation

You can have multiple selections open at the same time in PowerPoint. As you finish with some presentations, you may no longer need to have them open. You can close these presentations and continue to work in PowerPoint.

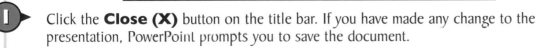

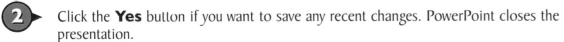

1 ▶ Click the **Close (X)** button on the title bar. If you have made any change to the presentation, PowerPoint prompts you to save the document.

2 ▶ Click the **Yes** button if you want to save any recent changes. PowerPoint closes the presentation.

 Ctrl+F4
As with most Windows applications, PowerPoint provides many opportunities to use the mouse when closing a presentation. If you prefer to use the keyboard for this task, you can press **Ctrl+F4** to close the active presentation.

End Task

Adding Presentations

PowerPoint gives you the chance to begin a new presentation each time you start the program, but you can create another new presentation at any time. For example, when you have saved and closed one presentation, you might want to begin a new one.

✅ **Default Filenames**
Depending on how many new presentations you have created while you are working in PowerPoint, the default filename for each new document (Presentation1, Presentation2, Presentation3, and so on) increases sequentially. When you exit and start PowerPoint again, the numbers begin at 1 again.

Task 9: Creating a New Presentation

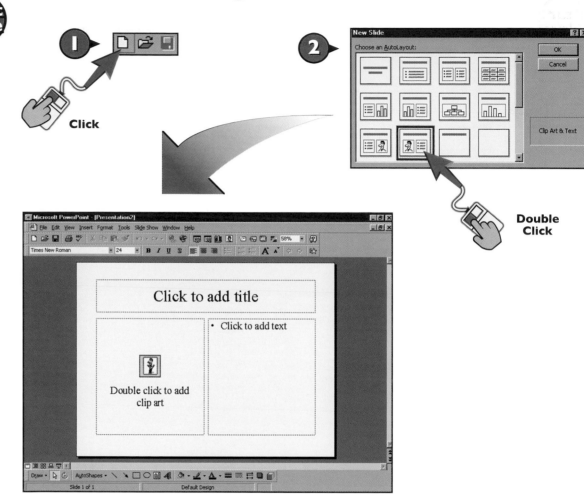

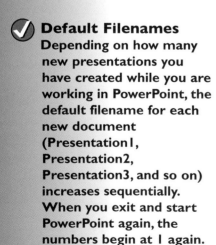

1 Click the **New** button on the standard toolbar.

2 Create the first slide by double-clicking its type in the **Choose an AutoLayout** selection area (for example, **Clip Art & Text**).

Task 10: Opening a Presentation

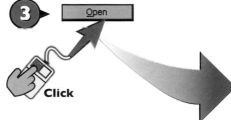

Click

Click

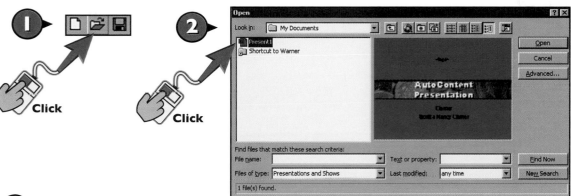

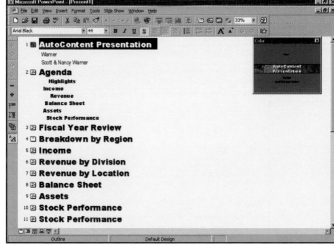

Click

Choosing a Presentation to Work With

Eventually, you'll have to close PowerPoint and any presentations you have created. If you saved your work, you can continue working at any time by opening the saved presentations. You also need to save your presentations so you can use PowerPoint to show your slides to others.

1. ▶ Click the **Open** button on the standard toolbar. PowerPoint opens the Open dialog box and displays the files that are currently saved.

2. ▶ Click the file you want to open (for example, **Present1**).

3. ▶ Click the **Open** button and PowerPoint opens the presentation.

✓ Opening an Existing Presentation

If you want to open an existing presentation and you just started PowerPoint, click Open an Existing Presentation on the PowerPoint opening dialog box to close the introductory dialog box options.

Saying Something in a Slide

After you create the presentation, whether by starting from scratch (refer to Task 2), using the AutoContent Wizard (refer to Task 3), or using a template (see Task 4), you need to put in the information you want to present.

Task 11: Adding Text to a Slide

Click

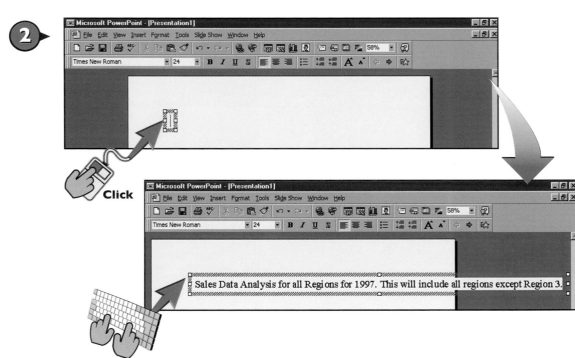

Click

> 1 Click the **Text Box** button on the Drawing toolbar.

> 2 Click the mouse pointer (which now looks something like an upside-down *t*) directly on the slide where you want to begin adding text. Type some text into the text box.

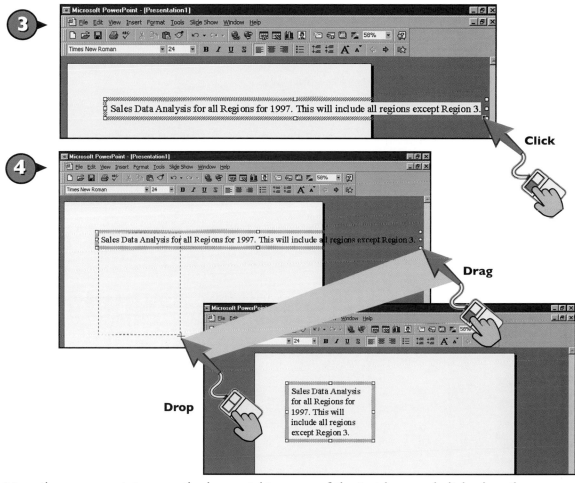

Click

Drag

Drop

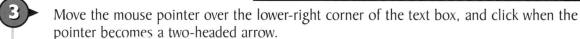

Adding Text in Outline View
Another way to quickly add text is to use the Outline view. This view enables you to add text without the clutter of other objects on your slide. Refer to Task 6 for information about using Outline view.

3 Move the mouse pointer over the lower-right corner of the text box, and click when the pointer becomes a two-headed arrow.

4 Drag the text box to the size you would like it to appear on the slide, and release the mouse button. The text inside the text box automatically wraps to the new size of the text box.

Task 12: Formatting Text

Applying Formatting

When you alter the format of your text, it is probably because you want to draw attention to certain information or show which text is most important. You can alter the formatting in your slide just the same as you did in a Word document or Excel worksheet.

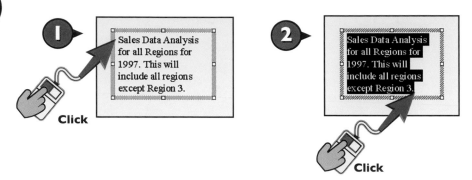

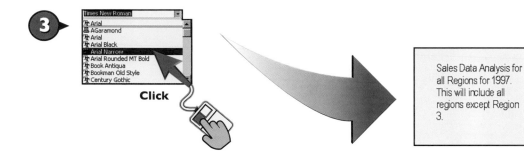

Start Here

Click

Click

Click

✓ **Selecting Text**
As in other Office 97 applications, you can double-click a word to select it or triple-click a word to select the entire paragraph.

1 ▶ Click the mouse pointer in the presentation at the beginning of the text you would like to format.

2 ▶ Select the text you want to format.

3 ▶ Click the **Font** drop-down arrow to alter the font (for example, choose **Arial Narrow**).

Next Step

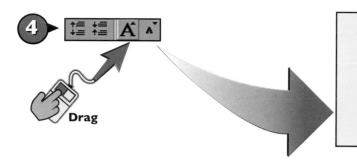

Sales Data
Analysis for all
Regions for 1997.
This will include
all regions except
Region 3.

Sales Data
Analysis for all
Regions for 1997.
This will include
all regions except
Region 3.

Text Box

If you click on the **Text Box** button on the Drawing toolbar and then select your formatting options before you click in the document, the formatting options you select become the default options. For specific information on the Formatting toolbar, refer to Part 3, "Working with Word Documents." Formatting options are similar in all Office 97 applications.

4 Click the **Increase Font Size** button to alter the font size (for example, click twice).

5 Click the **Center Alignment** button to center your text.

End Task

Task 13: Inserting Clip Art

Adding Graphics

Clip art adds visual interest to your PowerPoint presentation. With PowerPoint's *Clip Gallery*, you can choose from more than 1,000 professionally prepared images. Adding a clip art image is easy when you're using one of PowerPoint's AutoLayouts.

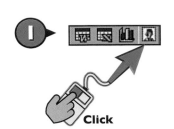

Click

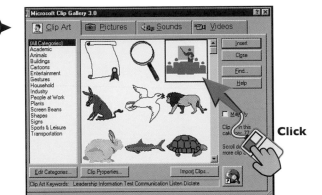

Click

Click

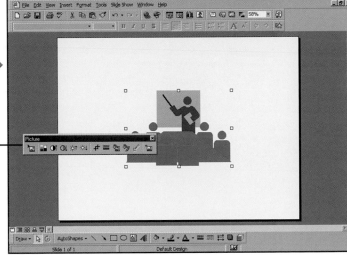

Picture toolbar

✓ **Picture Toolbar**

You can use the Picture toolbar to alter the clip art or click the **X** button on the toolbar to close it. To close the Picture toolbar automatically, click anywhere in the presentation area but not on the piece of clip art.

 Click the **Insert Clip Art** button on the Standard toolbar. Microsoft Clip Gallery 3.0 opens.

 Click the piece of clip art you want to insert.

Click the **Insert** button.

End Task

Task 14: Inserting a Word Table

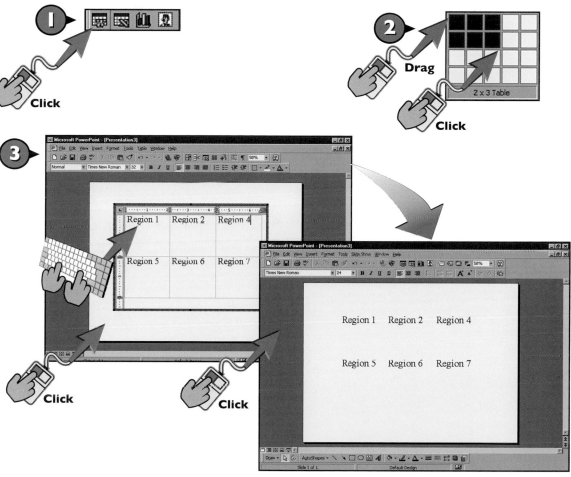

Click

Drag

2 x 3 Table

Click

Click

Click

Using Tables

Many times you need to add more to your presentation than just words. Maybe you want to display data or show relationships between numbers or totals. Creating a Word table in PowerPoint is one way to do this.

1 ▶ Click the **Insert Microsoft Word Table** button on the Standard toolbar.

2 ▶ Drag the mouse pointer over and click the number of rows and columns you want.

3 ▶ Type the text you would like to have in the table.

✔ Word Tables
If you forget how to move around a Word table, refer to Part 4, "Word 97 Tables." You can also copy and paste a table from Word into PowerPoint by using the Copy and Paste commands.

Task 15: Inserting an Excel Worksheet

Using Spreadsheets

Maybe you feel more comfortable working with Excel worksheets than with Word tables. In that case, you can insert an Excel worksheet directly into your presentation.

Start Here

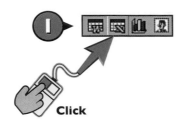
Click

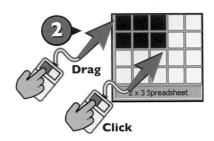
Drag
Click
2 x 3 Spreadsheet

Click

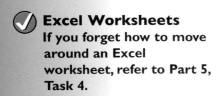

Excel Worksheets
If you forget how to move around an Excel worksheet, refer to Part 5, Task 4.

1 Click the **Insert Microsoft Excel Worksheet** button on the Standard toolbar.

2 Drag the mouse pointer over and click the number of rows and columns you want.

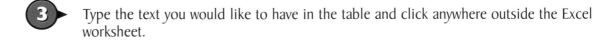
3 Type the text you would like to have in the table and click anywhere outside the Excel worksheet.

End Task

Task 16: Inserting a Chart

Start Here

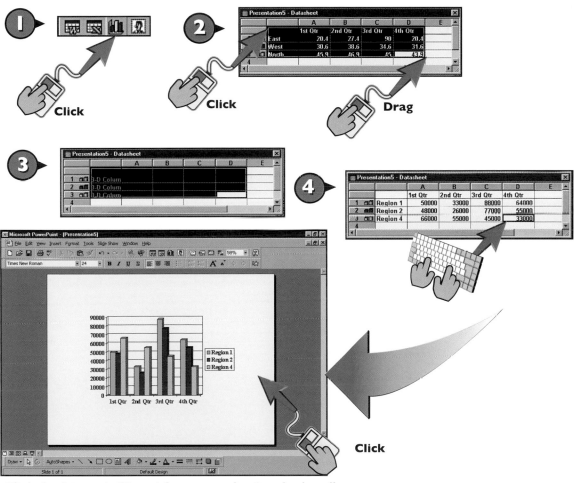

① Click

② Click

Drag

③

④

Click

Graphing Information

Charts can be one of the best ways to get your point across in a presentation because they present data visually. For example, instead of including a worksheet or table, you could use a graph that shows the comparison between your sales regions by quarter.

① Click the **Insert Chart** button on the Standard toolbar.

② Click in cell **A1** and drag the pointer to cell **D3** to highlight all the data.

③ Press the **Delete** button.

④ Type the data you want into the Datasheet and click anywhere in the presentation outside the chart.

✓ **Excel Charts**
If you forget how to work with Excel charts, refer to Part 7, Task 16.

End Task

Manipulating Objects

You can easily move or resize objects on the same slide, or you can move them to another slide. You can move and resize any object—text, art, a table, or a chart.

Task 17: Resizing or Moving Objects

Start Here

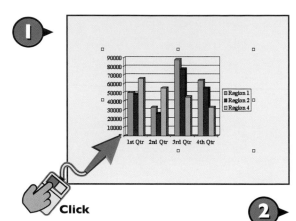

Click

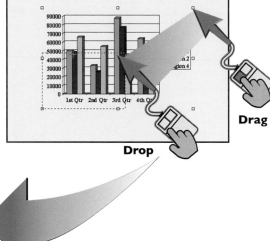

Drag

Drop

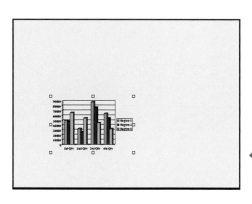

 Click directly on the object you would like to resize. Notice that **handles** appear around the edges of the object.

Click on a handle and drag the object to a new size; then release the mouse button.

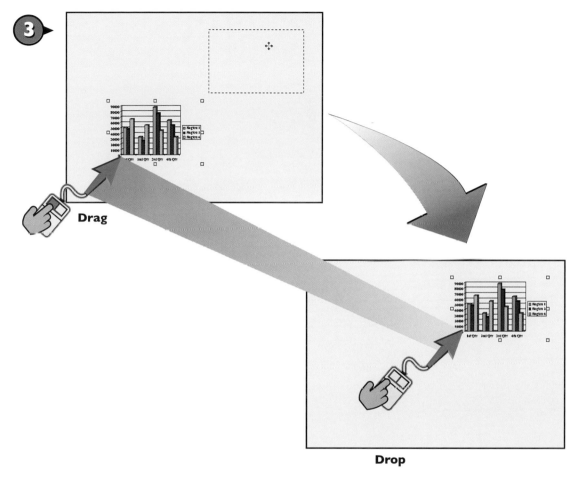

Drag

Drop

3 Click on the object. Hold down the mouse button and drag the object. Then release the mouse button to drop the object in a new location.

 End Task

✓ Keeping Correct Proportions

Using the corner border handles to drag the size of an object larger or smaller increases or decreases the horizontal and vertical size proportionaltely. If you use the side border handles, you increase the horizontal and vertical size separately, possibly making the object look out of proportion.

Task 18: Adding and Deleting Slides

Inserting New Slides

If you happen to think of a new topic you want to include in your presentation, you might need to insert a new slide. On the other hand, you might determine that your presentation runs a bit long and you need to delete a slide.

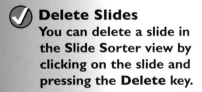

Delete Slides
You can delete a slide in the **Slide Sorter** view by clicking on the slide and pressing the **Delete** key.

Edit Menu
You don't have to be in the **Slide Sorter** view to delete a slide. You can choose **Edit, Delete Slide** in any view except the Slide Show.

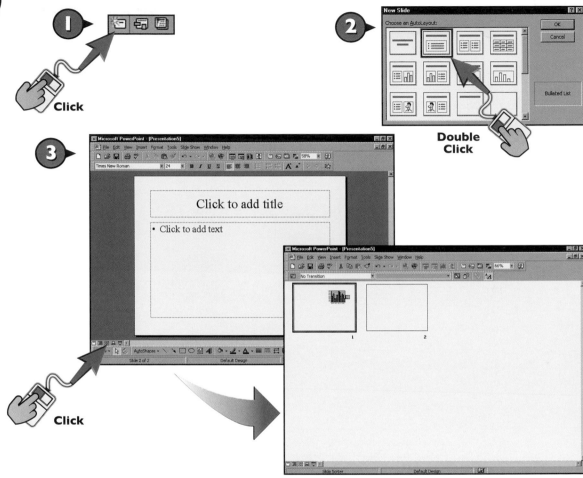

1 Click the **New Slide** button on the Standard toolbar.

2 Double-click on the type of slide you want in the New Slide dialog box (for example, **Bulleted List**).

3 Click the **Slide Sorter View** button to see the new slide you added.

Task 19: Changing the Slide Layout

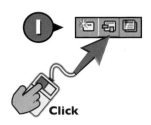

Click

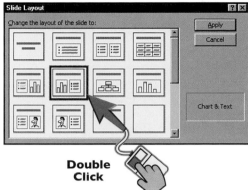

Double Click

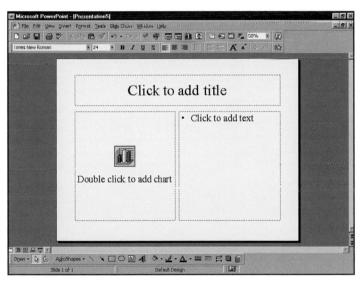

Applying Different Layouts to Slides

To add visual interest to your presentation, you can vary the layout of your slides. You can choose from 21 slide layouts (called AutoLayouts), including many that enable you to add visually interesting features such as clip art, tables, and graphs.

I Click the **Slide Layout** button on the Standard toolbar.

2 Double-click the type of slide you want in the Slide Layout dialog box (for example, **Chart & Text**).

WARNING
Try not to change the slide layout on a slide where you already have added information. This adds the AutoLayout on top of your current slide information. The best place to alter the layout is in a new slide.

Task 20: Changing the Slide Design

Changing the Look of Your Slides

Although you can alter the individual design of your slides, PowerPoint provides numerous designs you can immediately apply to your presentation.

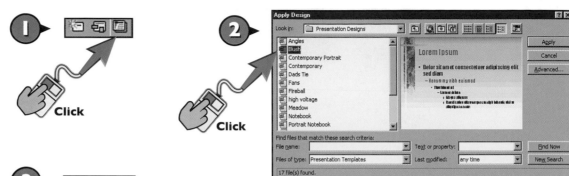

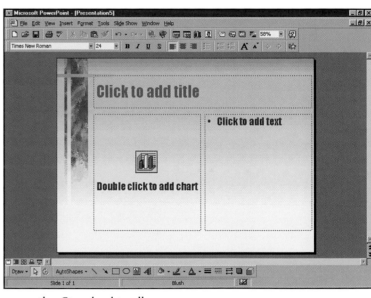

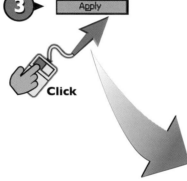

Start Here

① Click

② Click

③ Click

(!) WARNING

When you apply a design, keep in mind that it will be applied to all the slides in your presentation. If you apply a design after you have finished your slides, some of the design formatting might overlap some of the information on your slides.

① Click the **Apply Design** button on the Standard toolbar.

② Click the design you would like to apply from the **Presentation Designs** list box (for example, **Blush**).

③ Click the **Apply** button on the Apply Design dialog box.

End Task

Task 21: Reordering Slides

Start Here

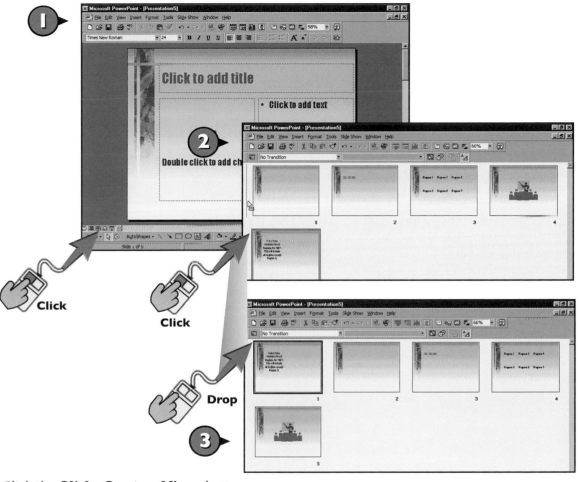

Click

Click

Drop

Rearranging Slides in Your Presentation

You can easily and quickly reorder the arrangement of your PowerPoint slides. For example, you might decide you want to place your graphical slides earlier in your presentation to draw the attention of the audience.

1 Click the **Slide Sorter View** button.

2 Click the slide and drag the mouse pointer to the desired location.

3 Release the mouse button to drop the slide in the new location.

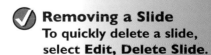
Removing a Slide
To quickly delete a slide, select **Edit, Delete Slide**.

End Task

Enhancing PowerPoint Presentations

When you finish creating your slides, you can add special features such as animation effects, transitions, and action buttons to enhance your presentation. In addition, you can type speaker notes and preview your presentation. You then save your presentation—your outline, slides, and notes—in just one presentation file, which you can easily open later and fine-tune the way you want.

With PowerPoint, you can print your outline, speaker notes, and audience handouts on paper. For a more professional-looking presentation, consider producing overhead transparencies, a computer slide show, or 35mm slides.

Tasks

Animating Objects

In today's multimedia world, text and graphics sometimes aren't enough to keep an audience's attention. PowerPoint's animation effects can bring presentations to life, making it hard for people to ignore information. You can apply animation to draw attention to especially relevant information.

Task 1: Adding Animation Effects

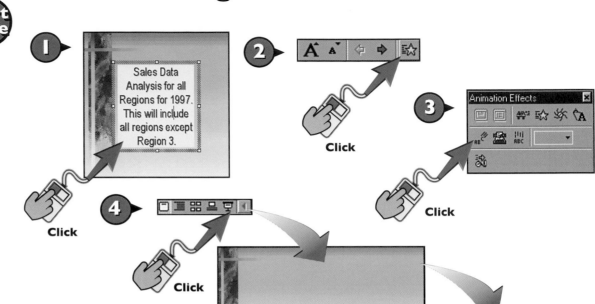

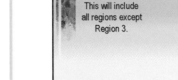

✅ **Applying Effects**
Animation effects are limited by the type of object to which you are applying them. For example, more effects are available for text than for a piece of clip art.

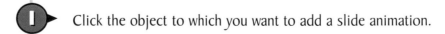

1 ▶ Click the object to which you want to add a slide animation.

2 ▶ Click the **Animation Effects** button on the Formatting toolbar.

3 ▶ Choose the effect you want to apply to the object (for example, **Laser Text Effect**).

4 ▶ Click the **Slide Show View** button and click on the screen to see what the effect will look like. Keep in mind that you need to press the **Esc** key to return to the Slide view.

End Task

Task 2: Adding Slide Transitions

Start Here

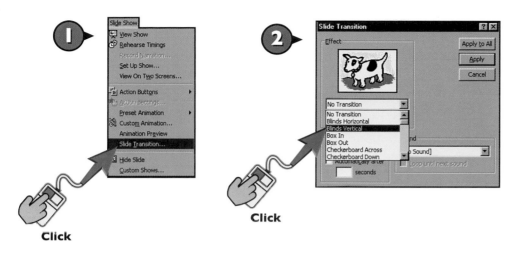

Click

Click

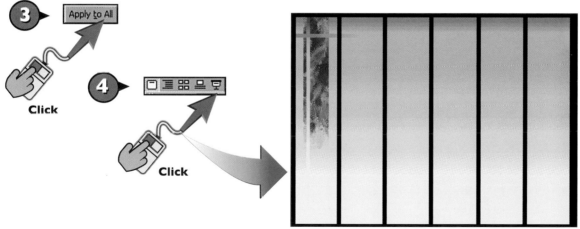

Click

Click

Setting the Look for Moving Among Slides

Slide transitions can make your presentations look more professional and interesting. For example, having each slide appear to open like a vertical blind draws the attention of the audience. For best effect, use only one kind of transition in a presentation—using more can distract the reader from your message.

1 Choose **Slide Show, Slide Transition**.

2 Click the **Effect** drop-down arrow in the Slide Transition dialog box and choose the transition you want to use (for example, **Blinds Vertical**).

3 Choose **Apply to All**.

4 Click the **Slide Show View** button to see what the effect will look like. Keep in mind that you need to press the **Esc** key to return to the Slide View.

✔ **Working with Effects**
You can select a different Transition effect for each slide by opening the slide, selecting the effect, and selecting to apply it to the slide instead of to all slides.

End Task

Working with Button Controls

Action buttons are special elements you can add to your PowerPoint presentations to provide information or draw attention to your presentation. You can set up any type of action: opening a document, linking to a URL, or even playing a sound or movie clip. For example, you can add an action button that makes a special sound when you click on a particular button during the presentation.

Task 3: Adding Action Buttons

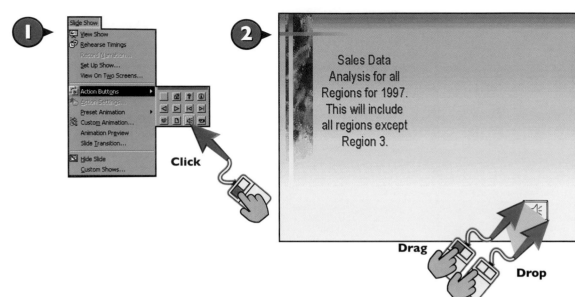

Click

Drag

Drop

Click

⚠ **WARNING**
Each action button should be independent of other objects on your slides. Action buttons will not work properly if you group them together.

1 ▶ Choose **Slide Show, Action Buttons, Sound**.

2 ▶ Click and hold the mouse button in the location where you want the action button. Drag to the appropriate size and then release the mouse button.

3 ▶ Choose **Yes** when a message appears, asking you to save your presentation. You should have already saved it previously.

Next Step

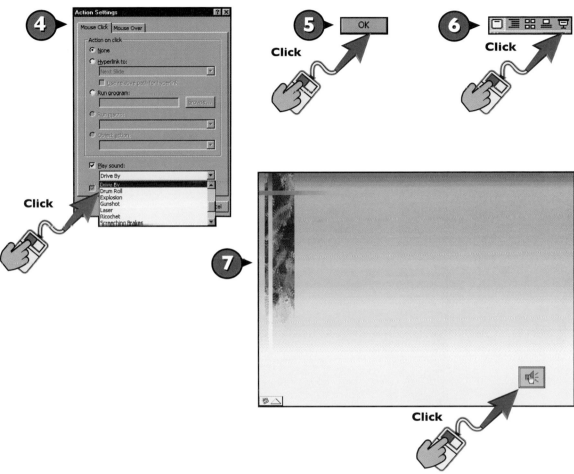

Click

Click

Click

Click

4 ▶ Click the **Play Sound** drop-down list box and select the sound you want to play when you click on the action button.

5 ▶ Choose **OK**.

6 ▶ Click the **Slide Show View** button to see what the effect will look like.

7 ▶ Click the **Action Button** to see how the action works. Press the **Esc** key on the keyboard to return to the Slide view.

✅ **Multiple Action Buttons**
You can place multiple action buttons on a slide.

End Task

Task 4: Adding Speaker Notes

Scripting Your Presentation

PowerPoint gives you room to type notes you can take with you to a presentation podium. *Speaker notes* are especially handy when you print them—PowerPoint reproduces the slide at the top of the page and prints your notes at the bottom. Use speaker notes to keep you on track while you give your presentation—they'll help you make sure you cover everything.

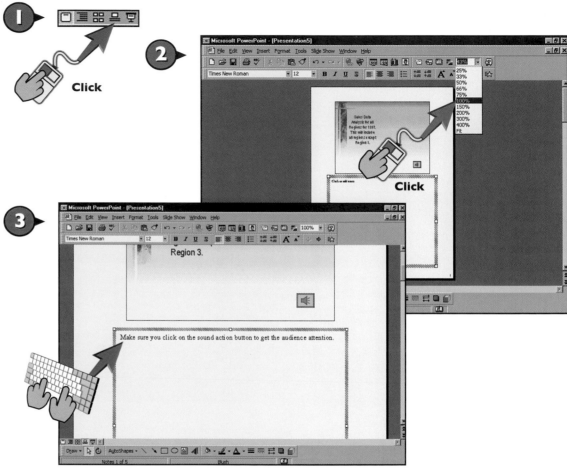

Click

Click

Region 3.

Make sure you click on the sound action button to get the audience attention.

✓ **Printing Notes**
Make sure you list the main points you want to cover in your speaker notes. This might include statistics or an anecdote. To learn how to print your speaker notes, see Task 7.

1 ▸ Click the **Notes Page View** on the View toolbar.

2 ▸ Click the **Zoom** drop-down arrow on the Standard toolbar and select **100%**.

3 ▸ Click in the notes area and type your speaker notes.

End Task

Task 5: Viewing the Slide Show

 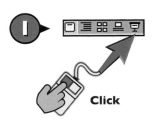

Click

Sales Data
Analysis for all
Regions for 1997.
This will include
all regions except
Region 3.

Looking at Your Presentation Onscreen

Perhaps the best way to test your PowerPoint presentation is to view the presentation onscreen. Your slides appear in vivid color and full screen (as they would in an actual presentation). You can use the mouse pointer or Page-Up and Page-Down keys to advance the slides and try any action buttons you have established. (Refer to Task 3 for more about action buttons.)

 Click the **Slide Show View** button on the View toolbar with your presentation open.

 Press the **Spacebar** to display the next slide.

 Continue to press the **Spacebar** until you have viewed the entire presentation. If you press the **Spacebar** on the last slide, the slide show ends. You can press the **Esc** key to stop the slide show anywhere in the presentation.

✓ Keyboard Options
To display the previous slide, press the Backspace key. To display a particular slide, press the specific slide number on the keyboard and press the Enter key. To stop the slide show, press the Esc key.

End
Task

Using Pack and Go

Perhaps someday you'll need to give a presentation using someone else's computer. If you're not sure PowerPoint is on that person's computer, you can create a Pack and Go presentation to view your presentation anywhere.

Task 6: Preparing the Presentation for Another Computer

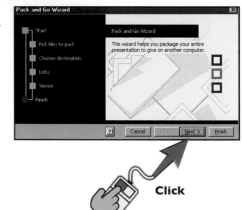

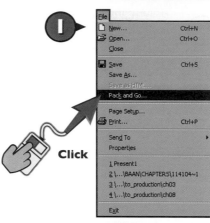

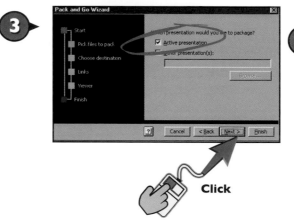

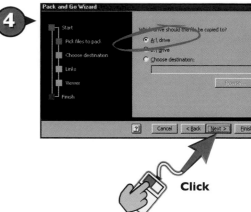

✓ Network Files

If your company allows you to place files on a network drive, and the conference room computer is connected to the network, you can access your files there.

1 ▶ Open the presentation you want to pack and choose **File, Pack and Go.**

2 ▶ Read the welcome information on the Pack and Go Wizard dialog box and then choose **Next**.

3 ▶ Click the **Active presentation** option and then choose **Next**.

4 ▶ Click the **A:\ drive** option and then choose **Next**.

Next Step ▶

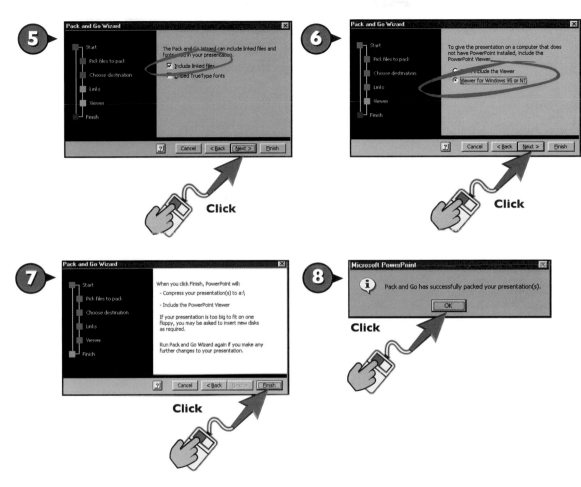

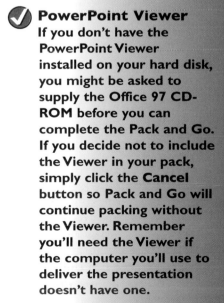

5 ▶ Click the **Include linked files** check box and then choose **Next**.

6 ▶ Click the **Viewer for Windows 95 or NT** option and then choose **Next**.

7 ▶ Read the Finish information, place a disk in the A:\ drive, and choose **Finish**.

8 ▶ Click the **OK** button when a message appears, letting you know the presentation was packed successfully.

Task 7: Printing a Presentation

Start Here

Getting Hard Copy

In PowerPoint, you can print different versions of your presentation as you need them. For example, you might want to print copies of your presentation so the audience can follow along, print your presentation in Outline view for your boss to review, or print speaker notes for yourself.

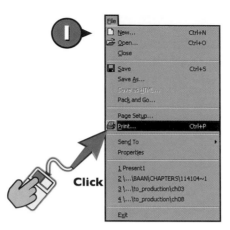

Click

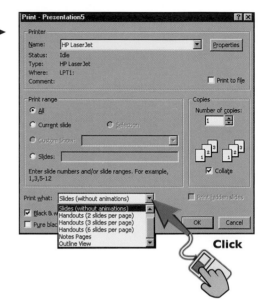

Click

Click

Additional Printing Options

In the **Print Range** area of the Print dialog box, you can choose to print all slides, the current slide, or specific slides. In addition, you can select the number of copies to print or have PowerPoint collate the slides.

Choose **File, Print**.

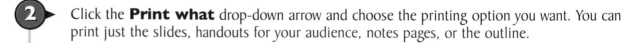
Click the **Print what** drop-down arrow and choose the printing option you want. You can print just the slides, handouts for your audience, notes pages, or the outline.

Click the **OK** button.

End Task

Outlook Basics

Microsoft Outlook is email, an appointment calendar, a journal, and other tools all rolled into one personal information management program. Outlook is similar to a three-ring bound organizer you might tote around during your business day.

With Outlook, you can keep track of email, daily appointments, and meetings. You can prioritize your work, and much more. Whether you are working on an individual computer or computers linked in workgroups, you can use Outlook to manage your time.

Tasks

Task I: Starting Outlook

Getting Started in Outlook

Outlook helps you manage your time and schedule using various tools. Whether you utilize all these tools or simply use Outlook for sending and receiving email, it will help you organize your daily communications. You might find it convenient to have Outlook open all the time in case you need to send an email or update a meeting time.

✓ Closing Outlook

As with all Microsoft Office 97 applications, you can click on the **Close (X)** button on the right side of the menu bar to close the application or, in the **Outlook** application, close an email message, note, journal entry, or task.

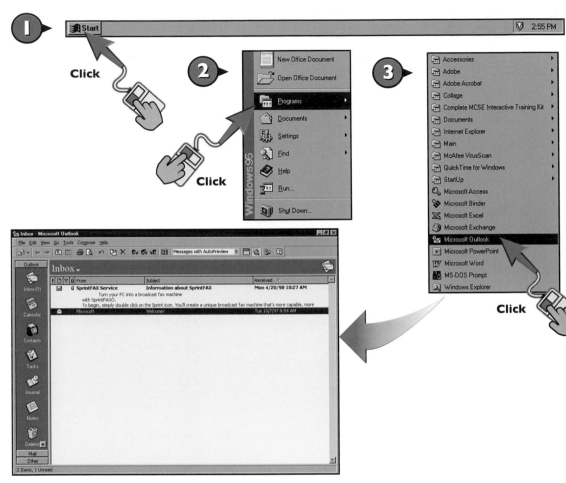

Click

Click

Click

Click the **Start** button on the taskbar.

Move the mouse cursor to **Programs**.

Click the **Microsoft Outlook** option and the application starts.

End Task

Task 2: Viewing the Mail Folders

Start Here

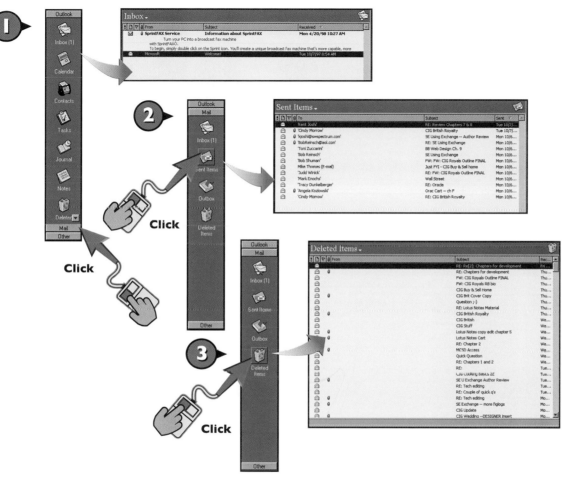

Working with Email Folders

Outlook manages many folders for your messages. For example, the Inbox enables you to send and receive email and faxes, preview messages before you open them, and mark messages with message flags to follow up on any action necessary.

1 Click the **Mail** group in the Outlook bar.

2 Click the **Sent Items** icon to display your sent messages, if you have any.

3 Click the **Deleted Items** icon to display your deleted messages, if you have any.

 Message Icons
An unread message looks like the back of a sealed envelope; a read message looks like the back of an envelope with the flap open.

End Task

Task 3: Opening and Closing a Message

Reading Email

You will find you need to open and close messages in the various Outlook Mail folders. You can open new messages, read messages, and draft messages.

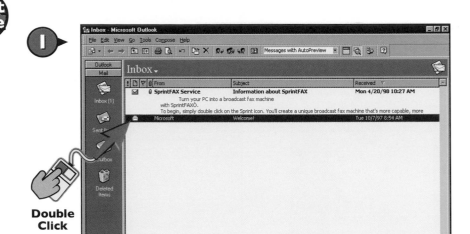

Double
Click

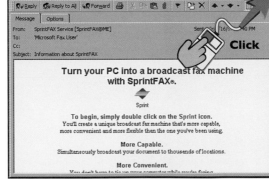

Click

✓ AutoPreview

Notice that after you open a new message, the AutoPreview of the first few lines of its text no longer appears in the main Outlook window.

✓ Multiple Messages

You can have multiple messages open at the same time. In addition, you can open each message to the maximum size by double-clicking on its title bar.

1 ▶ Double-click the message you would like to open.

2 ▶ Click the **Close (X)** button to close the message.

End
Task

Task 4: Saving Mail Attachments

Start Here

 1

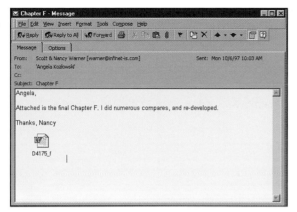

2

Click

What to Do When an Email Message Contains an Icon

Many times you will receive messages that contain attachments. These are usually files the sender wants you to use.

3

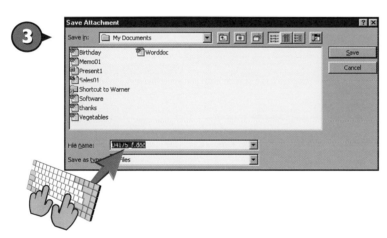

4

✓ Saving Multiple Attachments

You can save multiple attachments at the same time and to the same location. Outlook asks you which attachments you want to save to a particular location. If you want to save them one at a time to different locations, you can do that, too.

✓ Launching Attachments

You can double-click any attachment icon in the message to launch it. For example, you might do that if you just want to quickly view the attachment's contents.

1 ▶ Open an email message (Task 3 told you how).

2 ▶ Choose **File, Save Attachments**.

3 ▶ Type a name in the Save Attachments dialog box if you want to save the file to a different name.

4 ▶ Choose **Save**.

End Task

Task 5: Replying to a Message

Sending a Message Back

After you open and read a message, you will probably want to reply to it. You will usually want to add a sentence or two that explains why you're replying to the message.

Click

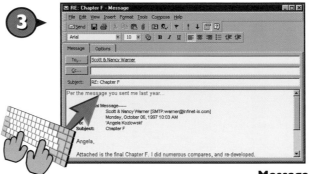

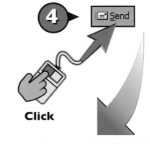

Click

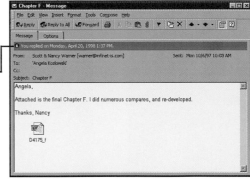

Message Information

End Task

✓ **Replying to Recipients**
You can reply to the person who sent you the message (the sender), to the sender plus additional recipients, or even to a completely different set of recipients.

✓ **Message Information**
After you reply to or forward a message, the original message contains a note that tells you when you replied. (For information about forwarding, see Task 6.)

1 ► Open an email message (Task 3 told you how).

2 ► Click the **Reply** button on the Standard toolbar.

3 ► Type your reply to the message.

4 ► Click the **Send** button on the Standard toolbar, and close the original message window (Task 3 told you how).

Task 6: Forwarding a Message

Start Here

1

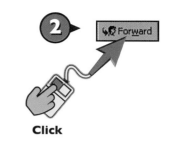

2

Click

3

4

Click

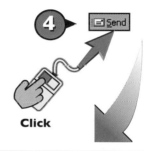

Message Information

Sending a Message to Someone Else

Sometimes when you read a message, you find that the information would be pertinent to another individual. In that case, you can forward the message to that person.

✓ **Original Message Window**
You can close the original message window by clicking the **Close (X)** button.

✓ **Replacing Information**
You can alter the information in the Message window by selecting the text and deleting it or typing over it. For example, you might want to alter the Subject line.

1 ▸ Open an email message (Task 3 told you how).

2 ▸ Click the **Forward** button on the Standard toolbar.

3 ▸ In the **To** box, type the email address of the person to whom you want to forward the message. Press the **Tab** key three times to begin typing the message.

4 ▸ Click the **Send** button on the Standard toolbar. Then close the original message window.

End Task

Task 7: Creating a New Message

Writing Email

Creating email messages is perhaps the most common thing you'll do in Outlook. Fortunately, creating a new message is not hard to do.

Start Here

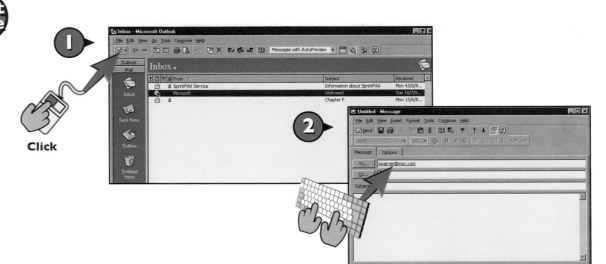

Click

Click

Click

✅ **Multiple Recipients**
To send a message to multiple recipients, simply place a semicolon between the email addresses. Another way to accomplish this is to click the **Select Recipients** button in a new message window, click on the recipients you want in the **Select Recipients** dialog box, and click the **OK** button. A semicolon automatically appears between the recipients.

① ▶ Click the **New Mail Message** on the Standard toolbar.

② ▶ Type the recipient's email address in the **To** box and press the **Tab** key twice (you can also add recipients in the **Cc** box).

③ ▶ Type a subject for the message in the **Subject** box and press the **Tab** key to enter your message.

④ ▶ Click the **Send** button on the Standard toolbar.

End Task

Task 8: Deleting a Message

Start Here

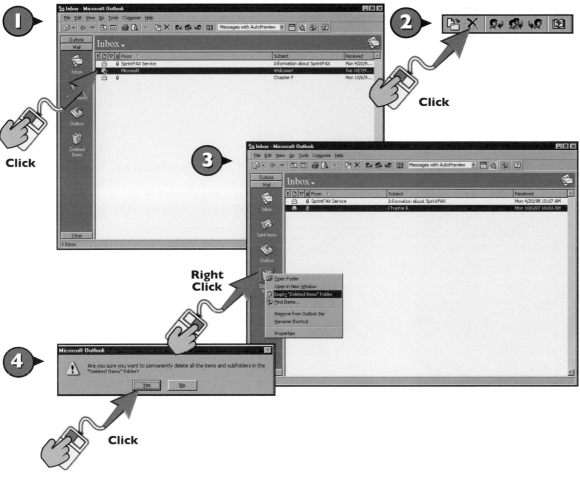

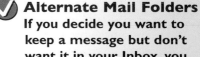

Click

Click

Right Click

Click

Getting Rid of Unwanted Messages

Just like regular mail, email has junk mail you will not want to keep in your Inbox. For example, you might want to delete the Welcome message Microsoft sends you the first time you use Outlook.

---

1 Click the message you want to delete.

2 Click the **Delete** button on the Standard toolbar.

3 Right-click the Deleted Items folder and choose **Empty "Deleted Items" Folder** from the shortcut menu.

4 Choose **Yes** on both message windows to permanently delete the message.

✅ **Alternate Mail Folders**
If you decide you want to keep a message but don't want it in your Inbox, you can click on the message and drag it into a different Mail folder.

End Task

Task 9: Viewing Your Schedule

Managing Appointments

In Date Navigator, you can switch the view from today's schedule to a different day, a week-at-a-glance, and a month-at-a-glance. You can schedule appointments and events in any view, as well as move the appointments and events.

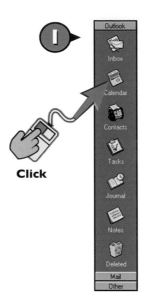

Start Here

1

Click

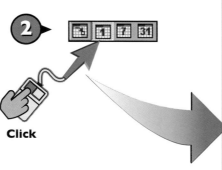

2

Click

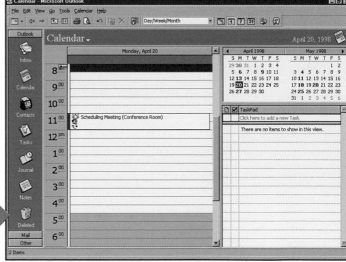

1 Click the **Calendar** button on the Outlook portion of the Outlook toolbar.

2 Click the **Go To Today** button on the Calendar toolbar.

Next Step

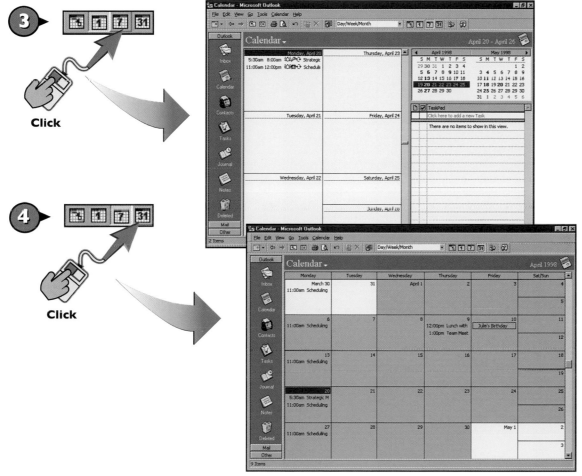

③ ▶ Click the **Week** button on the Calendar toolbar.

④ ▶ Click the **Month** button on the Calendar toolbar.

✓ **Long Appointments**
If your appointment is too long to read in the Week or Month view, click the **Day** or **Go To Today** button on the Calendar toolbar to read it all.

End Task

Task 10: Scheduling an Appointment

Adding Appointments

You can fill in daily and weekly appointments in your schedule. For example, you might want to schedule a meeting, doctor and dentist appointments, and conferences. The time schedule displays a 24-hour day, starting at 12 a.m. You can assign a reminder to an appointment so you don't forget about it.

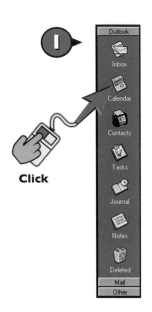

Click

Click

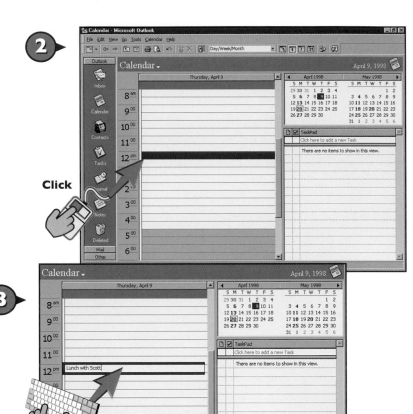

✅ **Move an Appointment**
To move an appointment to a different time slot, move the mouse pointer to the blue vertical bar on the left end of the appointment's or event's text. Drag the appointment or event to the new location.

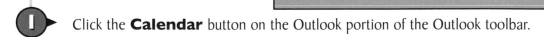

1 ▶ Click the **Calendar** button on the Outlook portion of the Outlook toolbar.

2 ▶ Click on the **12 p.m.** time slot in the Day view.

3 ▶ Type **Lunch with Scott** in the time slot and press the **Enter** key.

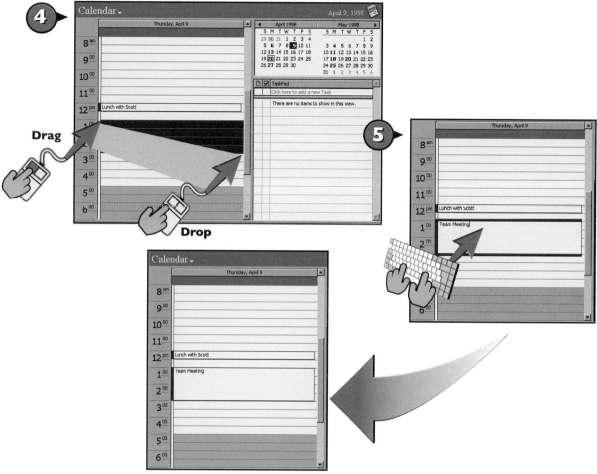

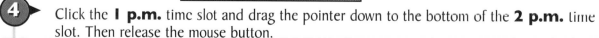

4 ▶ Click the **1 p.m.** time slot and drag the pointer down to the bottom of the **2 p.m.** time slot. Then release the mouse button.

5 ▶ Type **Team Meeting** and press the **Enter** key.

✓ **Remove an Appointment**
To remove an appointment, click on the appointment and click the **Delete** button on the Standard toolbar.

End Task

Task 11: Planning a Meeting

Inviting Others to a Meeting

Outlook's Meeting Planner enables you to plan a meeting from start to finish with other attendees. You specify the attendees, determine a meeting time, check for any schedule conflicts, and then schedule a room. You also can send a memo to the other attendees to invite them to the meeting.

Click

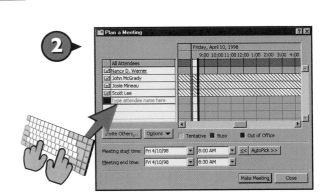

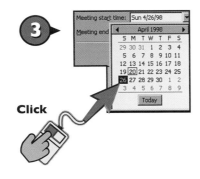

Click

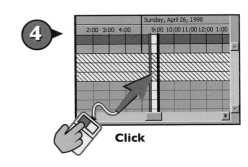

Click

WARNING

Keep in mind that you should offer meeting attendees alternate meeting times in case they have scheduling conflicts.

1 ▶ Click the **Plan a Meeting** button on the Calendar toolbar.

2 ▶ Type the name of the first attendee in the **Type attendee name here** text box and press the **Enter** key. Repeat this for each attendee.

3 ▶ Click a date in the **Meeting start time** drop-down list (for example, **Sunday**).

4 ▶ Click a **Meeting start time** in the time chart.

Next Step

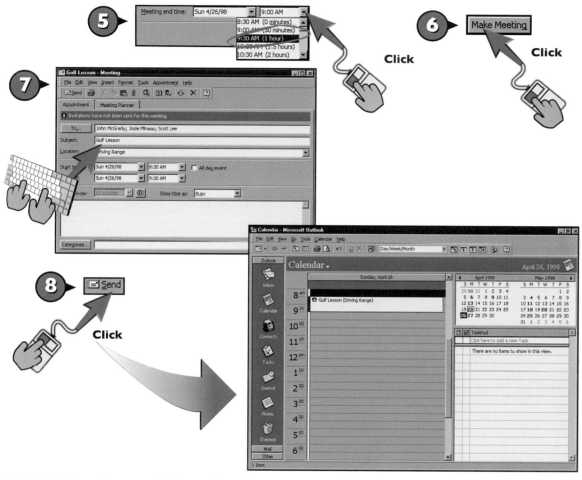

5 ► Click the **Meeting end time** drop-down arrow and drag the mouse pointer over the end time you would like to assign.

6 ► Click the **Make Meeting** button.

7 ► Type the meeting's title in the **Subject** text box, press the **Tab** key, and type where the meeting will be held in the **Location** text box.

8 ► Click the **Send** button on the Meeting toolbar.

✅ **Meeting Icons**
In the Calendar, choose the meeting's date on the current month calendar and then click the **Day** button on the Calendar toolbar. Notice the Meeting is scheduled, with a Meeting icon (two people) next to it.

End Task

Task 12: Creating a To-Do List

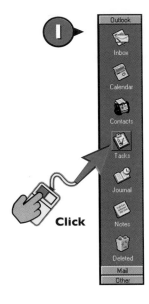

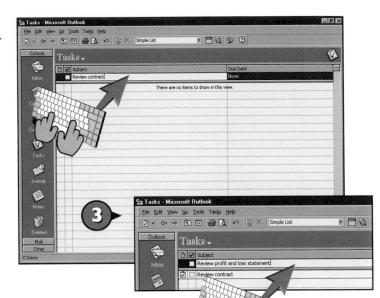

Managing Your Tasks

Creating a to-do list helps you organize tasks and projects significant to the dates and appointments on your schedule. You can build lists of daily things you need to do and items you must work on to complete a project. Any item you list in the to-do list is called a task.

Click

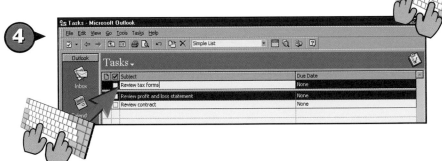

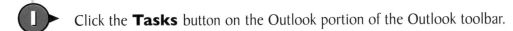

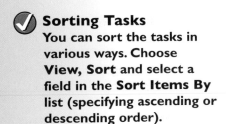

✅ **Sorting Tasks**
You can sort the tasks in various ways. Choose **View, Sort** and select a field in the **Sort Items By** list (specifying ascending or descending order).

1 ▶ Click the **Tasks** button on the Outlook portion of the Outlook toolbar.

2 ▶ Click in the **Click here to add a new task** box. Type `Review contract`, and press the **Enter** key.

3 ▶ Type `Review profit and loss statement` and press the **Enter** key.

4 ▶ Type `Review tax forms` and press the **Enter** key.

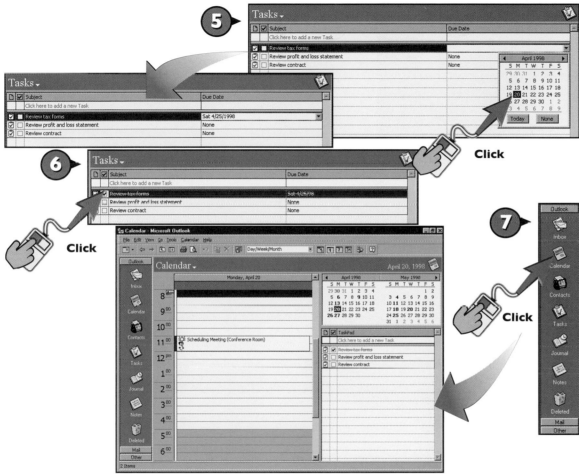

Click

Click

Click

5 ▸ Click the **Due Date** drop-down arrow next to any task and select a due date for that task.

6 ▸ Click the empty check box to the left of a task description. A line is drawn through the task, indicating the task is complete.

7 ▸ Click the **Calendar** button on the Outlook Bar to return to the Calendar view. The tasks are now listed on the *TaskPad* on the right side of the schedule.

✅ **Due Dates**
You don't have to assign due dates to your tasks, but doing so can help you keep track of when tasks need to be done and whether you have passed the completion date.

End Task

Task 13: Creating a Contact

Keeping Track of People

You can create a contact list that contains business and personal contact information. The list is an electronic version of an address book or card file. After you set up the names, addresses, phone numbers, and email addresses, you can use the contacts to create mailing lists and dial up other computers with a modem.

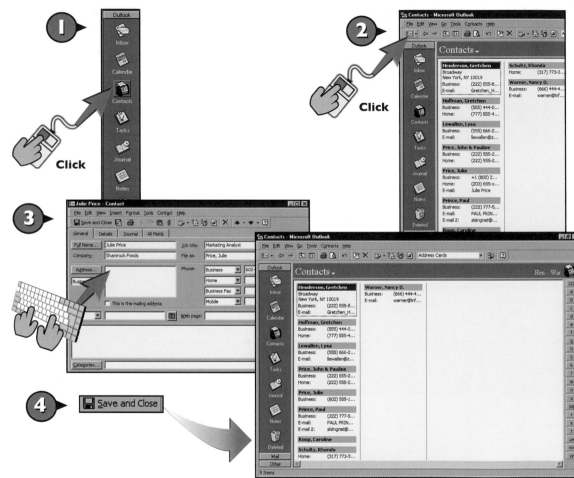

Start Here

Click

Click

Click

Save and Close

Delete a Contact
To delete a contact, click the contact to select it, and then click the **Delete** button on the Contacts toolbar.

1 ▶ Click the **Contacts** button on the Outlook Bar.

2 ▶ Click the **New Contact** button on the Standard toolbar.

3 ▶ Type the contact information, pressing the **Tab** key to move between text boxes.

4 ▶ Choose **Save and Close** on the Contacts toolbar when you finish.

End Task

Task 14: Creating Notes

Start Here

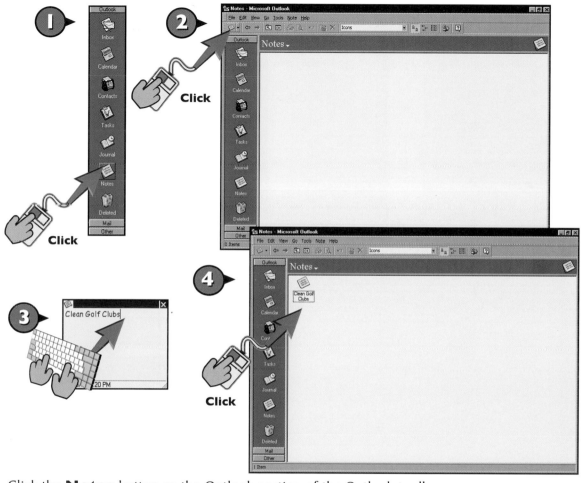

Click

Click

Click

Page 215

Working with Onscreen Sticky Notes

You can use Outlook's Notes feature to jot down ideas, questions, reminders, directions, and anything you would write on paper. You can leave notes visible onscreen as you work.

 **Open a Note in Note View**

To open a note in Note view, double-click the note. To resize an open note, drag the lower-right corner of the note. To delete an open note, click the **Note** icon in the upper-left corner of the note and then choose **Delete** on the shortcut menu.

---

1 ▶ Click the **Notes** button on the Outlook portion of the Outlook toolbar.

2 ▶ Click the **New Note** button on the Standard toolbar.

3 ▶ Type your note (for example, **Clean Golf Clubs**) in the Note box.

4 ▶ Click in the Notes window to see the note.

End Task

Task 15: Creating a Journal Entry

Tracking Activity

The Journal feature gives you one place in which to record information that is important to you. You can record activities such as talking to a contact, writing a mail message, or working on a file, as well as appointments, tasks, and notes. The Journal also automatically keeps track of work you perform in other Office applications.

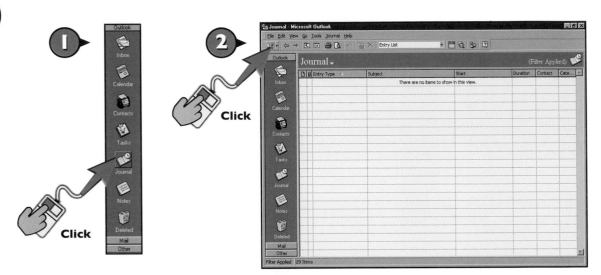

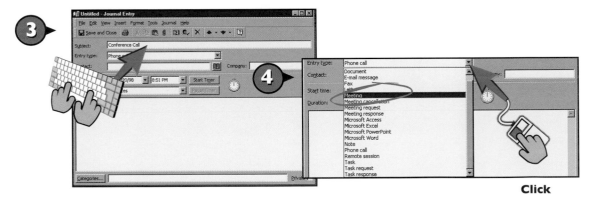

Delete a Journal Entry
To delete a journal entry in Journal view, right-click on the journal entry you want to delete and choose **Delete** on the shortcut menu.

1 ▶ Click the **Journal** icon on the Outlook portion of the Outlook toolbar.

2 ▶ Click the **New Journal** button on the Standard toolbar.

3 ▶ Type a subject (for example, **Conference Call**) in the **Subject** text box.

4 ▶ Click the **Entry Type** drop-down arrow to select the entry type (for example, **Meeting**).

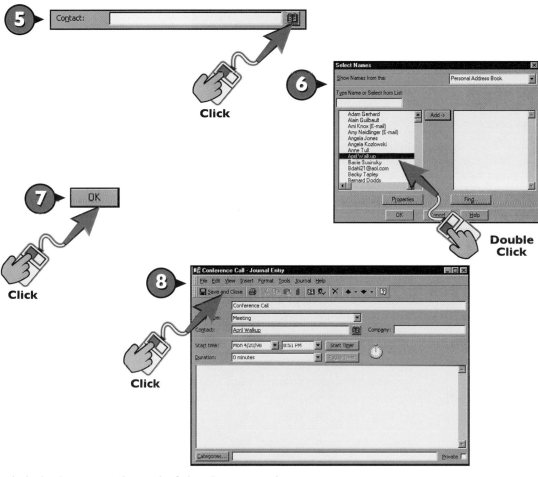

Click

Click

Double Click

Click

5 ▶ Click the button at the end of the **Contact** box.

6 ▶ Double-click the person's name in the Select Names dialog box.

7 ▶ Choose **OK**.

8 ▶ Choose **Save and Close**.

 **Timer Buttons**
The Stop Timer and Start Timer buttons enable you to track the duration of the journal entry (from beginning to end). That time duration is then displayed in the Duration list box.

End Task

Absolute cell reference An entry in a formula that does not change when the formula is copied to a new cell. In certain formulas, you might want an entry to always refer to one specific cell value.

Active document The document currently selected in your software window.

Alignment The way text lines up against the margins of a page. For example, justified text lines up evenly with both the left and right margins.

Animate To create the illusion of movement during a PowerPoint slide show by controlling how text is displayed.

AutoContent Wizard A tool in PowerPoint that guides you through the steps of a proposed presentation and includes suggested content.

AutoText Text that is corrected automatically. You can invent a string of characters that will automatically correct itself to a word or phrase. For example, Word comes with AutoText that automatically corrects "teh" to "the."

Bullet An object, such as a circle or square, used to set off items in a list.

Cell An area in an Excel worksheet or a Word table that holds a specific individual piece of information.

Chart A graphic representation of a selection of Excel workbook cell data.

Clip Gallery A collection of clip art, pictures, sound files, and video clips you can use to spruce up Office documents.

Color scheme A set of eight coordinated colors you can use in your PowerPoint presentation.

Column (1) In a table, a vertical set of cells. (2) In a document, the arrangement of text and graphics vertically so the document looks like a newspaper.

Conditional statement A function that returns different results depending on whether a specified condition is true or false.

Data The information you work with in an Excel spreadsheet, including text, numbers, and graphics images.

Datasheet A grid of columns and rows that enables you to enter numerical data into a chart.

Demote To indent a line of text more than the previous line, indicating a lower level of importance.

Dialog box Any of the information boxes that appear during the installation or use of an application and require input from the user.

Docked toolbar Any toolbar that is attached to one of the four sides of an application window.

Document Map A vertical display of the headings in a Word document. Click on an entry to move quickly to that part of the document.

Drag-and-drop To move an object (an icon, a selection of text, a cell in an Excel worksheet, and so on) by selecting it, dragging it to another location, and then releasing the mouse button.

Drop-down list A list of choices presented when you click the arrow to the right of a field in a dialog box.

Endnotes A Word feature in which a note number is placed within the document and reference information about the noted word or phrase is automatically placed at the end of the document.

File Information you enter in your computer and save for future use, such as a document or a workbook.

Filter A method in Excel for controlling which records are extracted from the database and displayed in the worksheet.

Floating toolbar A toolbar that is not anchored to the edge of the window, but instead displays in the document window for easy access. You can drag a floating toolbar to your Windows desktop.

Font The typeface, type size, and type attributes of text or numbers.

Footer Text or graphics that appear at the bottom of every page of a document or worksheet.

Footnotes A Word feature in which a note number is placed within the document and reference information about the noted word or phrase is automatically placed at the bottom of the page.

Format To change the appearance of text or numbers.

Formatting Applying attributes to text and data to change the appearance of information.

Function A built-in formula that automatically performs calculations in Excel.

Graphics Images that come in all shapes and sizes. Typical graphics include clip art images, drawings, photographs, scanned images, and signature files.

Handles The small, black squares around a selected object. You use these squares to drag, size, or scale the object.

Header Text or graphics that appear at the top of every page of a document or a workbook.

Highlight A band of color you can add to text by using the Highlight tool on the Word toolbar. In addition, when you select text to format or move, for example, you are selecting or "highlighting" the text.

Hyperlinks Text formatted so that clicking it "jumps" you to another, related location.

I-beam The shape of the mouse pointer when you move over a screen area in which you can edit text.

Insertion point The blinking vertical bar that shows where text will appear when you type. The insertion point is sometimes called a cursor.

Justification Aligning text so it fills the area between the left and right margins.

Macro A method of automating common tasks you perform in applications such as Word or Excel. You can record keystrokes and mouse clicks so they can be played back automatically.

Merge A feature that enables you to combine information, such as names and addresses, with a form document, such as a letter.

Mixed cell reference A single cell entry in a formula that contains both a relative and an absolute cell reference. A mixed cell reference is helpful when you need a formula that always refers to the values in a specific column, but the values in the rows must change, and vice versa.

Office Assistant An animated Office Help system that provides interactive help, tips, and other online assistance.

Page setup The way data is arranged on a printed page.

Path A way of identifying the folder that contains a file. For example, My Documents\Letters\Mom.doc means the document Mom.doc is stored in the Letters folder, which is stored in the My Documents folder.

PIM Personal Information Manager. Software (such as the Contacts folder in Outlook) in which you track information about contacts and keep notes on your interaction with those contacts.

Presentation A group of related slides you can create by using PowerPoint.

Promote To indent a line of text less than the previous line, indicating a greater level of importance.

Range A cell or a rectangular group of adjacent cells in Excel.

Reference Related to something in a specified context. For example, a formula referring to cell AI.

Relative cell reference A reference to the contents of a cell that Excel adjusts when you copy the formula to another cell or range of cells.

Replace A command on the Edit menu you can use to replace text with different text automatically. This feature can also be used with codes such as tabs and paragraph marks.

Row A horizontal set of cells in Excel.

ScreenTip Notes that display on your screen to explain a function or feature.

Search criteria A defined pattern or detail used to find matching records.

Select To define a section of text so you can take action on it, such as copying, moving, or formatting.

Shortcut key Keyboard combinations that provide quick ways to execute menu commands. For example, Ctrl+S is a shortcut key for File, Save.

Shortcut menu The menu that appears when you right-click an object.

Slide transition A special effect used to introduce a slide during a PowerPoint slide show.

Sort A function that rearranges the data in a list so it appears in alphabetical or numerical order.

Speaker notes Notes that help you document and give a presentation in PowerPoint.

Submenu A list of options that appears when you point at some menu items in Windows 95 and in applications designed for use with Windows 95. A small, right-pointing arrowhead appears to the right of menu items that have submenus.

Table A series of rows and columns. The intersection of a row and column is called a cell, which is where you type text and numbers.

TaskPad In Outlook, a list of tasks that displays when you use the Calendar folder.

Template Available in Word and Excel, templates provide predesigned patterns on which documents and workbooks can be based.

Workbook An Excel document that contains one or more worksheets or chart sheets.

Worksheet In Excel, the workbook component that contains cell data, formulas, and charts.

G

H

I

slide shows

Word

X-Y

Z